ACCELERATE

You!

"You've always had the power, my dear. You just had to learn it for yourself."

GLINDA THE GOOD WITCH, from *The Wizard of Oz*

ACCELERATE

You!

The power pivots,
mindsets, and steps to
power up your leadership

JERI CHILDERS PHD

Published by Grammar Factory Publishing,
an imprint of MacMillan Company Limited.

Grammar Factory Publishing
MacMillan Company Limited
25 Telegram Mews, 39th Floor, Suite 3906
Toronto, Ontario, Canada
M5V 3Z1

www.grammarfactory.com

Childers, Jeri.
Accelerate You! The Power Pivots, Mindsets, and
Steps to Power Up Your Leadership / Jeri Childers, PhD.

Paperback ISBN 978-1-998756-49-0
eBook ISBN 978-1-998756-50-6

1. BUS071000 BUSINESS & ECONOMICS / Leadership.
2. BUS109000 BUSINESS & ECONOMICS / Women in Business.
3. BUS107000 BUSINESS & ECONOMICS / Personal Success.

Production Credits
Cover design by Designerbility
Interior layout design by Setareh Ashrafologhalai
Book production and editorial services by Grammar Factory Publishing

Grammar Factory's Carbon Neutral Publishing Commitment
Grammar Factory Publishing is proud to be neutralizing the carbon
footprint of all printed copies of its authors' books printed by or ordered
directly through Grammar Factory or its affiliated companies through
the purchase of Gold Standard-Certified International Offsets.

THIS BOOK is full of my questions about personal power and how women design their lives, careers, and businesses. These questions are influenced and limited by my perspective as a white, cisgendered woman who has been advantaged by the systems that disadvantage women who are queer, First Nations, or differently abled, as well as women of color and those blessed with age—all of whom have a much greater chance of encountering high levels of discrimination. My perspectives in this book are meant to be helpful to people who identify as female. I am committed to continuing to learn, reflect, be challenged, and embrace change as we fight for a world that supports all people and their diverse intersectionality of gender, age, caste, race, ethnicity, class, sex, sexuality, religion, ability, weight, and physical appearance.

I would like to acknowledge the Traditional Owners of the land on which we connect today, and to pay my respects to the Elders past and present.

"Everything is within your power,
and your power is within you."

JANICE TRACHTMAN

CONTENTS

INTRODUCTION
UNLEASH YOUR
PERSONAL POWER

> "Tell me, what is it you plan to do
> with your one wild and precious life?"
> **MARY OLIVER**

THE WORLD OF work is changing. But do you have the power to change with it?

In the aftermath of the COVID-19 pandemic, and against a backdrop of global events with very real local impacts, the continuous need to navigate through uncertainty can leave you feeling depleted, lost, and, ultimately, powerless. In addition to external obstacles, there is an internal battle. Many people—women in particular—are experiencing a gap in their personal power. They want to make changes in their lives, careers, and businesses to create more meaning and purpose—but they lack the clarity, confidence, and certainty required to make those changes. Why is that?

In 2023, I reached out to women considering boosting their leadership capabilities, making a career change, and starting their own businesses. The majority of the women I surveyed indicated that they were experiencing one of the five personal power gaps that prevent women from reaching their goals. Power gaps exist when a person recognizes that something is missing in their life, career, or business that keeps them from experiencing the success, rewards, impact, or satisfaction they deserve, and they lose connection with their strengths, confidence, and personal power to overcome internal or external obstacles in their way to success and fulfillment.

The five damaging power gaps are:

1   Not recognizing your strengths (accomplishments, ambitions, abilities, attitudes, assertiveness, and authority) and your sense of your value and impact.

2   Letting your fear hold you back from acting or communicating with strength.

3   Failing to back yourself or to ask for what you require or deserve.

4   Being uncomfortable making decisions, solving problems, setting goals, or using or developing your resources.

5   Disconnecting from your strengths or isolating from influential support as you develop yourself

and lead others in the change you are creating.

How you see yourself and your personal power is a result of many things, including the culture you grow up in. Generally speaking, women have grown up facing widespread inequities that shape their sense of their potential. Culture can affect how you develop your unique leadership capabilities and how you learn to leverage your personal power for good.

Messages that shape women are everywhere—in nursery stories, children's toys, video games, social media, advertising, and throughout society. Girls and women of all ages and stages learn, and are shaped by, the traditionally limited view of their roles, capabilities, and contributions.

Too many organizational structures and cultures do not support diversity, equality, and inclusion. The majority culture, made up by those with the most power and privilege, negatively impacts women, and particularly women of color. Many workplace cultures create a context that inevitably limits women's beliefs about themselves and their capabilities, which leads to personal power gaps. If you work in a culture where you are in a minority, this work setting may be affecting your assumptions, perceptions, motivations, and behaviors, and, in many cases, can explain a power gap you might be experiencing.

Personal power gaps also emerge over time, starting with childhood experiences, and relate to the intergenerational beliefs, emotions, attitudes, behaviors, and influences from the family, school, and leaders who have raised and shaped you. These gaps come from the ways of being that you take on to feel safe and accepted.

In cultures throughout the world, girls are taught to be perfect, to please, and often to overperform to "fit in." This extends to adulthood, where women are pressured to act a certain way to maintain relationships, protect the status quo, and progress in their lives, careers, and businesses. Women often don't feel safe to stand out, express themselves, or ask for what they need. Many young women are encouraged to adhere to gender stereotypes that limit their aspirations, ambitions, and assertiveness. While girls and women achieve more and more, they are also filled with more and more self-doubt and anxiety—caring too much what others think of them.

This can lead to a feeling of powerlessness, which comes from judging yourself harshly, or unconsciously adopting harmful patterns of thinking and acting that derail your success and diminish your personal power. In trying to be perfect, to please others, to overperform, and feeling the pressures around you to conform, you lose a sense of what is important. You lose a sense of yourself, and you adopt strategies that are less than authentic and that are not aligned with your personal truths or values. Unconsciously, you don a mask, play a role, and give up pieces of yourself.

As women, it all feels exhausting and unfair—like the deck is stacked against us, creating a vicious cycle that erodes our clarity, confidence, and courage. It is time we identify and name what is holding us back and take steps to break this vicious cycle. We need to distinguish between barriers we build within ourselves, and those barriers built by social and organizational cultures designed by and for men. While the outside world plays a role in shaping you starting from your childhood, you can become conscious of your personal power gaps, and you can increase your connection to the personal power that you may have lost or given away.

Let me paint a picture for you. In many workplace situations, you may be confident and high performing, but there are moments when you are confronted with a triggering event or person and your reaction pulls you out of your personal power. For example, a new role, task, project, boss, teammate, or stakeholder can throw you off your game. You may have a tricky presentation or proposal to deliver. You may have been employed for most of your career and now you are the founder of a startup, making you the employer and not the employee.

In these moments of self-doubt, anxiety, and frustration, the context has changed, and suddenly and unexpectedly you are outside of your comfort zone. Momentarily, you are triggered, drained of your energy and internal resources to respond to the situation, and you may feel you've lost your clarity, confidence, and courage. You suddenly feel powerless. In these instances, you are temporarily out of your power zone and on a learning curve. You eventually level up and feel back in balance or more like yourself, but it's only a matter of time before you're knocked off your feet again.

Or perhaps it's more sinister than that. Perhaps you're working in a toxic culture or with toxic leaders where you may be dealing with discrimination, microaggression, bullying, unhealthy competition, isolation, gaslighting, a lack of mentorship or sponsorship, unfair treatment, or a lack of access to opportunities. These situations can be particularly triggering for those who have been traditionally marginalized, including people of color, immigrants, or women in male-dominated workplaces. How you and other women adapt to these cultures should be examined individually and collectively.

In these triggering situations, it is common for women to unconsciously choose strategies that they think will make them safe. Are you chronically overpreparing, overworking, or overperforming to fit in or to feel safe, secure, or successful? Are you keeping yourself small to avoid rocking the boat? These behaviors are coping strategies that are forms of self-sabotage that drain your personal power. These strategies are not sustainable and will not get you where you want to go in the long run.

Five power pivots

As I said earlier, the world of work is changing. If you, like many women, are ready to prioritize your passion, purpose, and yourself as you accelerate on your life, career, and business path, I encourage you to read on.

You may be frustrated with glass ceilings, locked out of opportunities, and tired of waiting for your turn to move up. Or you are looking inward to develop your own clarity, confidence, and courage to create your own "power plays." Whatever the case may be, you—and many women like you—are ready to accelerate ahead, pioneering your unique path forward and developing your own playbook for success— on your terms!

If this describes how you are feeling and what you want for yourself, the research-based, results-proven Accelerate You! framework—along with everything else you will learn in this book—will help you find and unleash your personal power, empowering you to make the necessary power pivots around the obstacles you are facing.

Think about it. Why are some women more successful than others in charting their life or career course, establishing their startup pathway, or building their business? Successful leaders define what success means to them and adopt powerful mindsets that help them leverage their personal strengths, which enable them to navigate an uncertain future. In other words, successful leaders have redefined their relationship with their personal power.

Are you tired of feeling stuck or feeling frustrated— and blocked from experiencing the success you desire? Do you want to experience more success and move more quickly and effectively toward your goals? If so, you will have to make these five power pivots:

- **Awaken** to your power to lead and to inspire yourself and others. Develop clarity around where you are going as you form the big picture. Let your personal vision pull you and others forward.

- **Activate** yourself and move toward your goals quickly and easily. Act and communicate from strength, not fear. Enjoy and thrive on the challenge of leading yourself through the transformation you want to see in the world. Adopt a growth mindset that makes the impossible possible, and which will fuel your self-confidence and inspire confidence in others.

- **Advocate** for yourself and your ideas. Ask for what is needed and what you deserve. Trust and back yourself and others. Demonstrate courage to leverage your inner wisdom to make decisions. Say "yes" to opportunities and say "no" when boundaries are important to keep your focus.

- **Amplify** your personal power, voice, and presence to influence others and be a force for good and positive change in the world. Become comfortable making decisions, solving problems, setting goals, and using or developing the resources required to create change. Risk, experiment, and collaborate to create your vision. Unleash your imagination and thrive on the innovative process.

- **Advance** yourself and others by measuring and celebrating your impact, achievements, and the change you have created in the world. Step up and marshal all the resources within your grasp to accelerate forward. Stand in your personal power, know your value proposition, and tell your story of impact in the world.

These five power pivots are a large focus of this book. In fact, each power pivot has an entire chapter dedicated to it. Later, I'll share a full overview of the contents of this book. But first, allow me to share my own power pivot story—and why I decided to write *Accelerate You!*

My power pivot story

The process of finding and unleashing your personal power keeps you vital. Your personal power or "juice" is your fulfillment and joy. Your life is always moving. When you are feeling stuck, it means you have lost your flow, which you will learn about in this book (including how to regain it). You can find or rediscover your juice and your personal power as you embrace and embody the positive changes you want to create in your life and in the world around you. This is what leaders and innovators do. Leadership is not just about a formal role or fancy job title. You must connect with your uniqueness and find ways to contribute to the changes that you want to lead within yourself, moment to moment, and the changes that our world so desperately needs.

My name is Jeri Childers, and I have experienced this process firsthand. Despite receiving a doctoral degree and achieving many of my career goals, I was feeling stuck and frustrated. I had lost my juice. I was in the United States during the global financial crisis, and I was at a crossroads looking for a new job and a new life. I felt like all the choices that I made to create a fulfilling life and to climb the career ladder had left me feeling exhausted, disillusioned, uninspired, and stalled. I had stopped learning, risking, being vulnerable, or being curious about what lay ahead for me. Instead, I was filled with fear. I had lost my connection with myself and my inner wisdom. I was frozen—afraid to change or lead change in my life— yet I knew that I needed a new job and a new life. I had awakened to the fact that time was passing me by and that I had regrets or yearnings that I couldn't explain. For the first time in a long time, I followed my heart and took a leap of faith.

About ten years ago, I took a job and came to Sydney, Australia with a single bag filled with all my possessions. I packed my bag for adventure. I was determined to live a life without regrets and wanted to design my life with more joy and meaning. My goal was to conduct an experiment that included starting up a new life, which I intended to fill with adventure, connection, and impact.

When I arrived, the first thing I did was go to Sydney Harbour and ask myself, "How do I start up this adventure-filled life?" I listened to my heart. I looked up at the blue sky and across the blue water to the

Opera House, gleaming in the sun, and over the Sydney Harbour Bridge. In the distance I saw the sail boats tacking back and forth on their way to the open ocean. The boats were pivoting—leaning toward the power of the wind and tide. They were navigating around the obstacles in their path with ease. They were in their flow. I could hear the buoyant voices of sailors calling out to each other with excitement and joy, and could see how they worked with the waves, the wind, and the moment to experiment until they accelerated. I had my answer. My first step in my new life adventure was to learn how to sail; this skill has served me well in all areas of my life and business.

Before I came to Australia, I didn't design my life around my passion, and I had lost my connection to my strengths and personal power. I had not awakened to my motivations and desires—my power or juice—and I had not faced the fears that were holding me back and preventing me from acting and communicating with strength. I was failing to back myself or to ask for what I wanted, needed, or deserved. With each step in my life, I felt like I was moving away from my fears instead of steering my life toward my goals. Most of the time, I didn't even realize that fears were stopping me. They were anchoring me in place and holding me down. Underneath those fears were emotional states like panic, anxiety, stress, and shyness. What I didn't know at the time was that deep in my subconscious, my fears were driving my life and career choices.

Early in my career, I was carrying around the values, dreams, and fears of my grandparents, parents, and teachers. I didn't know what I wanted, and I didn't have my own definition for success. Not only did I not take time to consider my desires and map out the many career destinations that would inspire me, I stayed too long in jobs that didn't challenge me. I waited for my supervisors to evaluate when I should be promoted or to tell me I was doing a good job.

I hadn't developed my own internal compass and didn't rely on my own intuition for decision making. I wasn't growing, risking, or planning inspiration in my life. I didn't design my life to be filled with love or joy. I was losing my connection to myself, my strengths, and those resources that could support me. I just pushed and pushed and was feeling stuck, undervalued, depressed, and burnt out. In short, I had disconnected myself from my personal power supply.

As I look back on the process of starting up my life in a new country, defining what I wanted in my life based on my deepest values and personal truths, and beginning to make the changes that were required to power up my life, career, and business, I had to understand the five power gaps that I was experiencing and make the five power pivots to get myself back on course. This process led me to understand the power of mindsets in personal, career, and business transformation.

Today, I apply best practices in career, leadership, and organizational development that focus on mindsets, culture, and what leaders must master to start up and scale up change in their lives, careers, and businesses. I began using the principles, strategies, and keys to success used by startups and scaleup founders in my life and career to improve my experience of my own personal power to lead change within myself and in the world.

I have used these steps for success with leaders around the globe, particularly with women leaders in the tech sector, many of them STEM researchers. These female leaders are inventing better methods to detect skin cancer, using robotics and AI technology to help the blind navigate the world more effectively, and improving physical rehabilitation with technology, to name just a few examples. These female navigators, explorers, and pioneers in their fields have contributed to the knowledge that I am sharing with you. These women feel a sense of urgency to create their vision and to advance and accelerate toward their goals. Today's women are tired of waiting for the world to change around them, and the world needs their leadership.

This book is a distillation of my years of research and professional practice into a framework to achieve success in life, career, and business. My passion is helping leaders create their vision and developing solutions that make their lives, careers, organizations, and the planet a better place. I have used these principles, strategies, and keys to achieve success in the classroom with engineers, IT professionals, data scientists, executives, and MBA students. I have been active in female leadership development, female founder mentorship, and business startup accelerators and incubator programs for the last fifteen years. The methods and masteries you will learn in this book come from my experience in coaching tech startups and helping researchers commercialize their ideas. I have had the privilege of working with founders at all stages of their startup and scaleup journeys, helping them gain clarity of vision, confidence, and courage to ignite their power of creativity, imagination, and innovation as they scale up their ideas to transform the world.

In each chapter of this book, you will discover the steps that you can take to power up your life, career, and business.

Five principles of *Accelerate You!*

This book will provide a process to increase your level of personal power and map out a pathway for you to reach your leadership goals. *Accelerate You!* is a framework for leadership development that provides strategies, powerful pivots, and the keys to successful authentic leadership. Drawing on startup methodologies, as well as enterprising and innovative mindsets from successful female leaders, this book will offer you resources to reframe your life, career, and business using core principles I have learned from accelerating thousands of leaders.

This book will model the methods of iterative, agile project management that leaders and teams can use to respond to uncertainty, risk, and complexity—progressing through a series of short, experimental pathways called sprints. Each sprint focuses on different requirements. During the sprint, leaders create a driving vision and roadmap toward their intended solutions, assessing the gaps, adjusting to the context, leveraging their resources and mindsets to close the gaps, and ultimately making powerful pivots toward their goals. I will be asking you to tap into the leader inside of you. You may not feel like a leader yet. I will be asking you to trust me and the process and watch the level of your personal power rise as you begin to "own" your leadership qualities.

Here are five principles to keep in mind as you embark on the path to *Accelerate You!*

1   **Become your own minimum viable product (MVP).** Embrace imperfection and think of yourself as a prototype or work in progress. Focus and master one thing at a time, creating, testing, and getting feedback on just the essential features of the change you are creating. This change could be as simple as bringing self-awareness into your leadership, or as complex as advancing in your career or designing a new product or service in your business. Focusing on your MVP enables you to confirm what is working and if there is a desire to scale up to a sustainable strategy for replicating your results and impact.

Release your inner perfectionist and embrace your MVP—appreciating the beauty of imperfection and accepting the process to find more freedom and growth.

2 **Disrupt yourself and reset your mindset for success.** Learn to own your roadmap, stories, emotions, and mindsets—and make choices that move you toward your goals. Learn what drives you forward and make the emotional and psychological investment to intentionally move out of your comfort zone. Understand the mindsets that support success and become agile at resetting your mindsets to reach your goals. This process will require you to uncover your passions, retrain your brain, and rewrite your own rules for your life, career, and business.

3 **Learn to establish your product market fit.** How well does your life, career, or business satisfy your needs and the needs of others? Are you designing your life, career, and business path based on your values? Does your life, career, or business "fit" you now? These questions can help you understand how things fit you now and whether they could fit you better in the future. How do you find your product market fit? Be curious. Explore what you want and need. Keep asking the questions because as you evolve and life changes around you, you may want to create a change to move closer to what you desire.

4   **Reclaim the runway of your life.** For startups, a runway is the amount of time you give yourself or you have available to achieve your goals. How long are you willing to wait to reclaim your life, career, or business? The clock is ticking. Do you want to live a life without regrets? Do you want to live an authentic life—daring to aspire, fail, and live on your own terms? Your private self and public self are collectively constructed. Be willing to reclaim the path and redesign your runway. Explore. Experiment. Know yourself, including what inspires and motivates you, and design a life, career, and business that reflects your values and desires. Learn to be playful and spontaneous and enjoy what comes. A well-lived life is filled with clarity, confidence, courage, creativity, connection, and celebration of each milestone. Commit to travel your runway with authenticity and integrity.

5   **Appreciate your strengths while continuously assessing the gaps, and pivot toward your aspiration.** Startups often pivot, change course, reboot, and reinvent their pathway—navigating around barriers, seizing new opportunities, and exploring different strategies for success. This process is normal and should not be tainted with judgments of "failure." Startup founders earn respect by owning their failures as badges of confidence, courage, and creativity. Pivots aren't seen as bad, but part of a process of tacking toward the winds

of change and opportune destinations, building momentum from all that you have learned previously. The process of appreciating, assessing, and moving toward your aspirations, like sailing the ocean, is simply charting your course from destination to destination in your life, career, or business. Once you commit to a pivot, you can set deadlines and measure your results. Having said that, you will be more productive and satisfied if you let go of the assumption that you need to fit into a predetermined mold or time frame. This process should be a creative and playful process in which you find your genius flow (more on this later). Give yourself permission to dream and explore. The process of powering up your leadership and designing your life requires you to own the change you want to create and to redefine your relationship with your personal power.

As you will discover, the *Accelerate You!* framework includes five mindsets, success strategies, and power pivots that can be deployed to help you achieve your goals. This process also requires monitoring progress, foreseeing obstacles, and pivoting around them. In this book, you will learn from other women the five damaging patterns that can derail you and how you can avoid them.

To orienteer this process, you will learn how powerful you are and how to raise your personal power. First, you must believe that you are powerful and learn the art of managing your mind and eliminating negative influences and distractions. Through my work with women seeking to better lead their lives, careers, and businesses, they have told me what they need to support their development. These women want to learn:

- How to find their strengths, purpose, and personal truths.

- How to embody clarity, confidence, courage, and creativity to develop their authentic leadership style to master change.

- The specific mindsets and strategies for success as they define it.

- How to chart their course on their own terms in uncertain waters and "hostile" environments.

- How to develop their personal power and make powerful pivots.

- How to give themselves the time and the permission to dream and define a life, career, or business that inspires them.

These are the key topics of this book. Read on for a full overview of the chapters that follow.

What you'll gain from this book

This book is written primarily from the point of view of how you, as an individual woman, can embrace your personal power for transformation. With so many women reporting that their employers are not investing in their development, women need their own tools and strategies. As a society, we are on the journey toward more diversity, equity, and inclusiveness for everyone, but women aren't waiting. No, this book isn't intended to fix women so that they fit into the inflexible spaces. Rather, it is intended to help women experience and step into their own power and leadership style with purpose and passion.

Use this book to learn about your personal power. Specifically, how to manage and grow it by learning how to assess your power gaps, and to make powerful pivots toward your goals. The chapters include research and brain science that you can harness as you power up your leadership. While this book was written based on the needs of female leaders in the tech sector, much of the research and best practice methods apply to what others are experiencing as well. Organizational leaders looking to advance and accelerate women will also find helpful information about what women need to support their growth. Each work system is different and has a unique culture. These cultures can be systematically measured, and strategies can be implemented to power up all leaders at each level of the organization.

Here is an overview of each chapter of this book:

- In Chapter 1, you will learn about personal power, including why it is important, what it looks like, sounds like, and feels like to experience your personal power and your power gaps, and how to harness and manage your personal power to reach your goals.

- In Chapter 2, you will learn the power of your mindsets as a determiner of your success, and you will understand how you can reset and retrain your brain to help you reach your goals.

- In Chapter 3, you will learn the five damaging patterns that drain your power. You will also learn how to assess and address your power gaps.

- In Chapter 4, you will discover the five power strategies and five power pivots you can make to power up your leadership in your life, career, and business.

- In Chapters 5 through 9, you will find each of the five power pivots explained in detail, including examples for each power gap in your life, career, and business, the mindset that you can use to close the gaps, the power pivots that you will have to make to power up your leadership, and strategies and keys to success that can guide your power pivots. These five chapters—and the reflective questions and affirmations included in each—will enable you to create your own personal power playbook. Accelerating yourself toward your goals is an iterative process. For each power pivot you take in your journey, you will repeat the five steps to *Accelerate You!*

- At the end of the book, we'll explore the framework that I use with my clients and partners to advance and accelerate female leaders. Your personal power playbook will include the pivots, strategies, and pathways that you curate based on what you learn from this book. You are designing your individual pathway using your own leadership style, based on your context.

Are you ready? Let's get to it.

CHAPTER 1

POWER UP YOUR LEADERSHIP

"When you're in your power, you make
an impact not by reacting to the behavior
of people who are limited, but rather by
raising yourself and others to be limitless."
SHARON MELNICK, PhD

Y OU ARE READING this book because you want
something more in your life, career, or business
and you want it now. You don't want to take the
slow lane; you want to accelerate forward. You are
ambitious and you want success more consistently,
and you want to define success on your own terms.
You can't wait for the world to change, and, in fact,
you want to be part of the solution. Yet every day you
wake up and face a world that seems so unfair, potentially leaving you feeling even more powerless.

Every day you face difficult challenges, and you find it harder to experience joy, happiness, and the success you deserve. You ask yourself, "Why is it so hard to confidently face the day? What is missing?" The missing ingredient is your personal power to create the change you know is required to experience more happiness and success. I am talking about the power to experience these five parts of yourself:

- **Clarity** that comes from connecting to your strengths and being inspired.

- **Confidence** that comes from letting go of negative influences, emotions, or beliefs that hold you back from acting, communicating, or setting bold goals.

- **Courage** to back yourself and your decisions to ask for what you require or deserve.

- **Creativity** to imagine, innovate, experiment, collaborate, and problem solve.

- **Choice** to cultivate and celebrate change and personal transformation, reflect on your evolution, and tell yourself and others the stories of your value and impact in the world.

Before coming to Australia, I had reached a point in my career where I experienced so many internal and external barriers to moving forward that I was exhausted and burnt out. I had no energy, and very little inspiration or clarity on the goals I wanted to set for myself. This left me feeling stalled, like a boat in the middle of the ocean without the power of the wind. I had confidence in my abilities and strengths but was feeling anchored in place by the work culture I found myself in, and the fact that my voice and vision were not valued. My ambitions for myself and my work style didn't fit the traditional culture where I was employed. Facing these external barriers to my leadership day after day wore me down. I lost my connection to my personal power, and it just leaked away slowly. However, I decided to make a change. I surrounded myself with a trusted crew of supporters and created a safe space to rebuild my energy and personal power. This process required that I identify my power gaps—where I was leaking my power—and close those gaps by adopting new mindsets, strategies, and power pivots.

In this chapter, you will discover the importance of your personal power. I have shared with you the voices of women I have worked with who experienced these moments of reckoning and were able to make powerful pivots to regain their personal power and accelerate toward their goals. Included here is research and resources that I think will be useful for you on your journey to create the changes you want to make in *your* life, career, and business.

What is personal power?

Martin Luther King Jr defined personal power as the ability to achieve one's purpose and to effect change. Personal power is the ability to inspire and influence change. Being in your power or powering up your leadership means that you manage your mental, emotional, and physical states. You are making choices, moment to moment, to be a force of good in your life. What unlocks personal and business outcomes is the knowledge of how to move into and stay in your personal power.

You can reframe your relationship to your personal power, and learn to unlock and contain your personal power, to accelerate your results and achieve more consistent success.

Julie Diamond, in her book *Power: A User's Guide*, defines power as energy and a human drive to shape the world, influence others, and make impact. Your personal power is the ability to positively impact your life and the lives of others around you.

Sharon Melnick, PhD, in her book *In Your Power*, refers to personal power as an energy that leaders emit that brings themselves and others into win-win solutions. She states, "Being in your power is the ability to alchemize the challenging aspects of what goes on outside of you to get 'into a good place' inside of you so that you can then take actions to achieve your aims and make the situation as you envision it."

Kathy Caprino, in her book *The Most Powerful You,* refers to personal power as the ability to "make the changes that can transform our lives … to experience more strength, confidence, authority, and impact so that we can overcome the obstacles in the way of success and fulfillment."

Why is personal power important?

The keys to success are managing your energy or personal power that fuels your clarity, confidence, courage, and creativity, and the ability to cultivate, lead, and manage change. If you want to achieve your goals, you must learn how to move into your personal power and close any power gaps that leak your self-esteem and confidence and undermine your vision for yourself. To accelerate yourself and to power up your leadership, you will need to know and name your power, as well as be able to contain your personal power, and not let it leak away. You will need to transform your relationship with power by learning how to connect with it, maintain it, and use it to change yourself and the world.

HERE ARE SOME OF THE VOICES OF WOMEN WHO HAVE LOST THEIR CONNECTION TO THEIR POWER.

"I have lost my confidence, and I am overwhelmed and filled with anxiety."

"I feel like my emotions are controlling me. I am hijacked, I can't focus, and I can't respond in the moment."

"I feel unchallenged, unhappy, disillusioned, disappointed, filled with fear, and I don't know what is next for me, so I do nothing and find myself staying too long in work roles and relationships that are unsatisfying or non-supportive."

"I am a good performer and get results. I don't ask for help or ask for raises or promotions. I believe if I work hard, they will notice me, and I will be promoted. I don't like to 'toot my own horn,' but I am tired of waiting for them to recognize and reward me, and I am tired of being seen as the 'work horse.'"

"I feel invisible, even though I am constantly working late. I make it look easy, yet I have lost my balance, and I am burned out. I am not progressing in my career, and I don't know what to do next."

"I have plenty of ideas that will bring in revenue, bring down our costs, and provide better customer service. However, when I pitch my ideas, nothing happens."

You can hear in these women's voices their feelings of powerlessness, frustration, loss of energy, and dwindling hope. In these examples, the women were not standing in their power, or they were pulled out of their power by their situation, beliefs, emotions, mindsets, or behaviors.

When you are pulled out of your power, a situation or context, another person, or something within yourself determines how you react, behave, or feel about yourself. You are pulled out of your power when you feel less like the cause in the situation and more like the casualty. To determine if you are being pulled out of your power, ask yourself these questions: Are you reacting? Are you being triggered? Are you being hijacked? If the answer is "yes," you are being pulled out of your personal power. In contrast, you are in your power zone when you are conscious of your state of mind, feel in control of your perceptions and responses, and are anchored in your power to create a win-win relationship between your mindsets, actions, and behaviors.

Fortunately, you can leave behind any mindsets, patterns, habits, and triggers that no longer serve you and step into the highest version of yourself to recover the personal power you were born with. You can realize the truth about yourself—you are resilient, capable, and possess limitless potential.

What does it look like to be in your power?

When you are in your power, you are connected to your vision and purpose, confidence, effectiveness, resilience, mental wellbeing, and impact. Being in your zone of power helps you see, cope, and change the injustices that continue to exist in our workplaces and in our communities, and act as an agent of change.

What do you look like and feel like when you are in your power? You are:

- **Calm, clear-headed, and focused**. You are awake to your mental wellbeing and resilience.

- **Confident and an active problem solver**. You know that you can handle anything that comes your way, and you are not letting your fear hold you back.

- **Courageous, results-focused, and making a difference for yourself and others**. You back yourself and your decision-making abilities, often advocating for yourself and the needs of others.

- **Creative—innovating and imagining the possibilities of a better future**. You create what is needed and solve problems as they arise. You change what is broken, inefficient, or unjust in creative ways.

- **Cultivating and celebrating the transformation, evolution, and impact**. You advance yourself and others by reflecting, reframing, re-visioning, and leveraging your results. You know how to lead change. You know how you are unique and different, and you know the difference that you make in the world. You know that you are a power for good.

Many of us were not raised to celebrate ourselves, to be responsible for our own evolution or impact, but we can learn the self-mastery that comes with emotional intelligence, and we can awaken to our personal power and use our personal power for good. Kemi Nekvapil, in her book *Power: A Woman's Guide to Living and Leading Without Apology*, describes her process of redefining personal power and the need for women to give themselves permission to use their power. Embracing your power is a process and a journey. Give yourself permission to power up!

Female leaders are reclaiming their relationship with their personal power. Forward-focused organizations aiming to advance and accelerate women in the workplace are developing leaders to be more conscious, authentic leaders who activate their personal power for good. The word "power" is often associated with manipulation, selfishness, and abuse. However, when you unpack the term, you will see the Latin root of the word "power" means "to be able."

Our negative perceptions about power come from traditional forms of leadership that are being challenged and replaced with the art of modern leadership in which the role of the leader is one of change agent, entrepreneur, and innovator, requiring the leadership qualities of clarity, confidence, courage, creativity, and the ability to lead, manage, measure, and celebrate change in times of uncertainty. To possess and leverage these essential ingredients within yourself will require you to have self-awareness, and to consciously raise your energy and your personal power to create change and to lift everyone around you. Think of personal power—and clarity, confidence, courage, creativity, and leading change—as the yeast in the recipe of leadership.

Leaders who are connected to and leveraging their personal power for good influence their peers and foster a positive worldview. They are assertive, respectful, successful, humble, driven, and stable. People with personal power effect change within themselves and with others around them by regulating themselves—displaying self-trust and inspiring trust. Contrast this way of being with those leaders in positional power that effect change by regulating others. Someone who is clear and confident in themselves will connect and influence those around them without the need for positional power.

Your personal power can come from your interpersonal skills (called referent power) and can be seen when you are approachable, put others at ease, listen to others, and inspire others to act, commit, and have confidence in their ideas. This power is linked to your ability to motivate yourself and motivate others toward goals.

Personal power cannot be given to you and is not the same as external sources of power (called legitimate or positional power). Leaders with positional power may be playing an important role but they do not necessarily inspire others, or foster cooperation, creativity, or emotional engagement in others, unless they leverage the personal power that comes from developing and using interpersonal skills. The best leaders build and use their personal power for more effective and sustainable results.

Personal power can also include what you know (called expert power). When you build up expert knowledge in specific areas or demonstrate a capacity to solve problems, leverage technical skills consistently, make good decisions quickly (often with imperfect data), and can gather and marshal resources effectively, you are demonstrating your personal power.

There are aspects of personal power that you cannot see but you can experience them in yourself and leverage them for good. Your personal power comes from within and is your intentional, energetic presence. You can learn to own and manage this power, presence, and influence.

The elements of personal power at your command

The building blocks of personal power require you to be conscious and able to command your agency, authority, abilities, and attitudes. Remember, personal power is the ability to influence yourself and others. This form of power comes from within; it's not an external, formal authority that comes from a role or position within an organizational structure. Personal power is having a strong connection to your inner resources and personal truths, which can be tapped to enable you to survive and thrive. As I describe each of these elements of personal power, consider where you might want to build your capability to power up your leadership.

Agency

You have a strong sense of agency when you know yourself to be the creator of your life, career, or business. As you take increasing responsibility in these three realms of your life and you become a more conscious leader, you become aware of and "own" your thoughts, feelings, reactions, and actions—and know that you consciously choose your responses to situations. You see yourself as proactive, not reactive. You know your values, beliefs, perceptions, and preferences. You are in control of your thoughts and behaviors, and their consequences. You can focus, filter what is essential, and find emotional and physical balance to advocate for yourself and others. Personal agency is important to managing your wellbeing, happiness, and success.

Authority

You stand in your personal authority when you consciously choose to believe in yourself and give yourself permission to lead your life, career, and business. Each moment, you are either writing or rewriting the narratives of your life. You own your stories about who you are. You decide if you are worthy, able, and enough. You know your personal truths, your purpose, where you will take your stands and why. You have a deep connection to your vision and your values and make good choices for yourself and the common good. You take actions and communicate confidently without fear. You have found your voice, and you use it for good. You trust yourself and your opinions. You take the time to explore, name, and know what you need and want. You know you have the right to change directions and change your mind. You know that you're continually evolving and that your aspirations and ambitions can change. You can set priorities and boundaries and ask for assistance when you need it. You assume responsibility for yourself and others and are committed to setting and achieving your goals.

When you stand in your authority as a leader, others around you are influenced by your clarity, confidence, courage, and creativity. You see yourself as an agent of change with the ability to imagine, innovate, invent, and influence others to collaborate and cocreate with you. You are capable and comfortable to build coalitions for good. Each of us, regardless of our situation or role in life, is a leader and knows examples of how we influence ourselves and others without any formal authority. As women, we may not always enjoy the politics of life or our workplaces, but we know it is important to constructively influence others for good.

Ability

You know your abilities to effect change or to create an intended result. You appreciate that you have more to learn but you feel able to take on the world. You believe in yourself and your abilities. You know the difference you create. You are confident that you can control your behavior and are responsible for your intended outcomes. You see yourself as an instrument of good and that you can effect change in yourself and others. You can see the big picture, the possible solutions, and create or cocreate the best possible solution for all involved. You believe in your resourcefulness and your persistence. You have a strong connection to your personal power to connect, create, collaborate, and cooperate with others to create positive change. You experience your *power in* your self-awareness, your *power with* others as you influence and lead dialogues, collaborations, and cocreations, and your *power to* solve problems and innovate new ways of work. You don't use your *power over* others.

Assertiveness

You communicate with others directly, honestly, respectfully, without fear, and without intention to hurt their feelings. You know that direct communication can increase clarity and reduce conflicts, anxiety, and stress. You communicate your needs, wants, feelings, beliefs, and opinions. You are comfortable and confident in defending your point of view or presenting the information required for effective decision making. You respect both your needs and the needs of others.

Attitude

You know your attitudes or motivations. Attitudes are preferences or patterns of thinking, feeling, believing, or emoting that are often a result of your past experiences, which influence your behaviors. Your attitudes are mental states that you know you can change. Attitudes are also called mindsets. You are aware of your mindsets and have the flexibility to adjust or choose mindsets that will make you successful in different situations. The next few chapters will explore mindsets in more detail, and how you can use mindsets to increase your personal power and your leadership capability in a variety of situations.

Ambition

Ambition is not a personal trait or a fixed quality. Ambition is a strong desire and determination to achieve a goal for yourself or others. Ambition is important because your aspirations or ambitions motivate you and focus you. Ambitions ebb and flow. They can feel stronger at different times in your life. You can learn how to be ambitious or to grow your ambition, which is important because without ambition you wouldn't be able to work toward your goals. Ambition is that sense you may have of wanting to excel at something or that feeling you have when you are doing something you love. When you are ambitious, you are persistent, have a vision, and want to make a difference for yourself, for those around you, and for your community. Ambition can be measured and increased (if that is your desire) and is linked to the motivations and capability for goal setting and goal achievement. Associate Professor Oksana Barsukova, PhD, has identified characteristics of ambitious people. These characteristics relate to your attitudes to set and achieve goals, your attitudes about yourself and others, as well as your attitudes about self-regulation. Think of ambition as the fuel in your tank that powers you to motivate yourself and others. Ambition also can drive your willingness to take risks or move forward despite your fears.

The term "ambition" has some negative connotations. Much has been written about the gender ambition gap and women's levels of ambition. Anna Fels, in her *Harvard Business Review* article titled "Do Women Lack Ambition?", explored the myth of a gender ambition gap. She found that depending on the context and the stage of life, ambitions for men and women are similar. However, women experience different personal, cultural, and organizational barriers compared to men, and define their ambitions differently and make different choices compared to men. Katie Abouzahr and her colleagues, in their Boston Consulting Group article titled "Dispelling the Myths of the Gender 'Ambition Gap,'" found that women start their careers with similar ambition levels as men and, although ambition levels vary, the biggest contributor to low levels of ambition are the organizational cultures in our workplaces. When organizations create positive, flexible, and nurturing cultures supporting gender diversity and inclusion, women have strong levels of ambition. The good news is that your ambition level is within your control if you choose to power up your leadership.

How to find your personal power zone

Spoiler alert! Power doesn't come from who you know, what you do, what you own, how you look, or how much money you have in the bank. It comes from unconditional love you have for yourself and from embodying your talents and gifts. Your personal power—your zone of power—is defined by your personal truths that nurture you and form the foundation of your life force. Your personal power zone is bounded by your personal truths. Knowing your personal truths is essential to authentic leadership and forming your own leadership style. When you embody your authentic leadership style, you will be more satisfied, productive, and effective. Anchoring your personal truth in your body and your mind is as necessary as having a compass, GPS system, or chart to map your current location and your destination. It requires clarity, and the ability to see the big picture and the steps required to achieve your goals.

Your personal power consists of your level of clarity, confidence, creativity, and courage to stand in your personal truths. To embody your personal truths daily, you need to answer these questions:

- What do I appreciate about my strengths, ambitions, and motivations?

- What gives my life meaning and purpose?

- What do I value and want?

- What are my boundaries?

- What are the problems I want to solve or the changes I want to make in this world?

- What is my personal definition of success and how will I measure my success?

- How can I become more conscious, intentional, and authentic?

The answers to these questions become the foundation of your personal truths and the standards by which you will measure yourself. Without knowing your personal truths, you have no way of knowing whether you are growing, evolving, or contributing to the world. Without asking these questions, you will not experience your inspiration, energy, motivation, momentum, or life force. When you know your truths, you establish for yourself and the world that you respect yourself and others. Knowing your personal truths is imperative to maintaining and raising the level of your personal power. Getting to know your personal truths is one of the most important steps you can take to accelerate yourself toward your goals. When you stand in your personal truths daily, you will be inspired, guided, and prosperous in your life, career, and business.

Your truths are your compass and your barometer as an authentic leader. Managing your personal power levels is part of your self-care routine and is a requirement of accelerating you toward your goals. If you are like most people, you move in and out of your personal power zone moment to moment, unconsciously. When you learn to monitor and manage your personal power, you can stay in your personal power zone longer. When you are in this zone, you experience a "flow" state. Mihaly Csikszentmihalyi, in his book *Flow: The Psychology of Optimal Experience*, describes the traits, benefits, and ways of finding your flow state. When you feel focused, happy, strong, empowered, and engrossed in the moment or activity, you are in your flow state or power zone. These moments will make you feel alive, satisfied, and productive. Getting into and staying in your flow enables you to experience more energy and results. Learning to power up is learning how to move into your flow to accelerate and sustain your personal power and your results.

To accelerate yourself forward toward your goals, it is important to find your personal power zone, as well as the strategies that put you into and keep you in that zone. Equally important is your ability to quickly learn the patterns or ways of operating that draw you out of your power zone or those situations where you leak your power. To identify this power zone, start by asking yourself these personal power questions to assess if you are containing or leaking your personal power.

PERSONAL POWER ZONE QUESTIONS	PERSONAL POWER ZONE	NO-GO ZONE
	CONTAINING YOUR POWER	LEAKING YOUR POWER
CLARITY MINDSET		
Am I operating from my strengths? (Abilities, ambitions, accomplishments, attitudes, agency, and authority)	Yes	No
Am I designing my life, career, and business in alignment with my life's purpose?	Yes	No
CONFIDENCE MINDSET		
Am I making my choices and decisions based on my values?	Yes	No
Am I acting and communicating without fear?	Yes	No
COURAGE MINDSET		
Am I backing myself in my decision making?	Yes	No
Am I creating healthy boundaries?	Yes	No
CREATIVITY MINDSET		
Am I comfortable making choices, leading, expressing myself, and leveraging resources when the outcome is uncertain?	Yes	No
Am I inspiring myself and others to imagine and innovate to add value?	Yes	No
CHANGE MINDSET		
Am I connecting within and with others to create, celebrate, and sustain change?	Yes	No
Am I developing myself to be a more conscious, intentional, and authentic leader?	Yes	No

Your answers will help you begin to understand the mindsets you use naturally and those you may want to develop to close your power gaps. If you answer "yes" to these questions, you are taking personal responsibility to manage your personal power zone. You are setting yourself up for success as an authentic leader and powering up your leadership. When you keep your energy and personal power reserves high, you are in a better position to achieve your goals. If you answered "no" to these questions, you are at a choice point. You can decide to close a gap, build your mindsets, and develop a roadmap to achieve your goals. Or you can stay where you are. Refer to these questions regularly because the answers will change!

Creating your personal power container

As you form your intent to increase your personal power reserves, it is equally important to focus daily on creating the container that holds your personal power. This container fuels your mind, body, and spirit connection to your personal power, which enables you to tackle your goals. This container holds the space for both your personal power and your positive energy, and can define a boundary from the fears, limiting beliefs, and turmoil that come with daily life.

During this transformational journey, you will be challenged, shaken, scared, exuberant, and confident. You must learn to hold yourself with self-compassion and to contain your personal power. You must learn to trust yourself—your intuition and your choices. To create your personal safe space and build your container, you must be willing to:

- Recognize your strengths and accomplishments and be willing to rewrite your personal narrative as you evolve, grow, and gain more insight into your abilities, value, the progress on the changes you are making, and the impact you are creating.

- Create an inspiring vision of what success looks like for you that fuels your ambition and motivates you toward your goals.

- Be clear on your goals and plan for achieving your definition of success, which inspires your confidence and courage to navigate beyond real and perceived barriers.

- Know your personal truth and watch your confidence and courage increase in the face of adversity, which can boost your decision-making and problem-solving ability, increase your motivation to achieve, and reduce stress.

- Be self-aware and embrace all aspects of yourself, which amplifies your self-trust, confidence, and resilience, and can increase your levels of satisfaction and happiness at each stage of your leadership development journey.

- Know and befriend your emotions—they are indicators of your thoughts, beliefs, and dreams, and can reveal areas where you feel conflicted, fearful, or powerless.

- Learn to reflect and reframe your personal assessments of yourself and your progress, and bring to the surface buried or unconscious emotions, beliefs, influences, or patterns that limit you. Start by noticing when your inner critic calls your choices into question. Look out for damaging ways of thinking that hold you back and begin to advocate for yourself by reframing any thoughts, beliefs, and emotions that block your momentum. More on this in later chapters.

- Consciously make loving choices for yourself and others.

- Back yourself—reference your own authority and intuition when you make decisions, asking for help or for what you deserve.

- Communicate clearly and without fear.

- Stay present under stress and soothe yourself in healthy ways when you are upset and scared.

- Choose to positively influence yourself and others as you develop win-win solutions to complex problems.

- Measure, manage, and describe the positive change you create to motivate yourself and influence others.

- Surround yourself with supporters—recruit your support team and allies.

Building your container for your personal power and your personal truths is essential to accelerating and powering up your leadership. This will call you to know your passion and purpose, which is referred to as your mission or your "why." Margie Warrell, PhD, describes a process for this in her *Forbes* article titled "Do You Know Your 'Why?' 4 Questions To Find Your Purpose." Building your container to hold your personal power will help you build your self-awareness and find your personal truths. Coming later in the book, you will learn a process for finding and naming your personal truths.

How do you power up?

To begin the next steps in your journey of transformation, choose one or more goals for powering up your life, career, or business. Begin to consider your current relationship to your personal power and learn about how you embody your personal power. Then move on to monitoring and managing your personal power. This will require you to reconnect with the sources of your personal power. To get started, here are some questions you can ask yourself:

- What does it feel like to be in my power and what pulls me out of my power?

- What mindsets can I adopt to shift into my power?

- As I raise my power and learn to manage my personal power for good, what is the problem I am solving in my life, career, or business?

- What is my purpose for making a change for myself and those around me?

- What steps or pivots can I make to shift back into my power zone?

- How does my level of personal power contribute to the solution I want to create?

- What is the specific change I want to achieve within myself to solve the problem?

These questions require you to have a sense of your personal power, and how you tap into and manage your internal resources to raise your power and to motivate yourself and others to get the results and impact that you are seeking.

I came to Australia to live my life differently—without fear and regret. I made a conscious choice to challenge myself to step up and take responsibility for my life, even when there was the possibility of failing, or I felt like retreating into my comfort zone or giving up altogether. When I chose to learn how to sail, I was excited about the idea of sailing, but I was also afraid. However, I learned to stand in my personal power, living true to what I wanted for myself, what I believed, and what was important to me. I asked myself the questions I just shared with you and connected to my power source—acknowledging all that I was capable of, and knowing and accepting who I was; the good, the bad, and the ugly.

This challenge, and others that I chose for myself, required me to live and speak with authenticity and truth, and to make choices that felt right for me. I advocated for myself and was committed to my self-discovery and growth, setting boundaries and rules to live by that prevented me from giving my power away. Here are some of the things I've learned about standing in your personal power:

- Identify your values and what is important to you. Know what you believe in and what lifts you up.

- Set boundaries. These boundaries are essential to protecting your personal power, and help you communicate your needs and protect your time and energy.

- Practice self-care. Put yourself first and prioritize your needs because it helps you be confident and energized.

- Speak your truth. Be honest with yourself and others by expressing yourself authentically and without fear of judgment.

- Be proactive—don't wait for others to make things happen for you. Remaining proactive will help you move toward your goals and dreams.

When I learned to sail, there was so much to learn. I hated the discomfort of being a novice, making mistakes, or letting the crew down during a race. I kept with it because I knew the experience of sailing was teaching me so much about myself and helping me step into my personal power. It took time and practice, and it was worth it. I learned that stepping into my power was a journey and not a destination.

When you stand in your power, you outwardly project your strengths, accomplishments, abilities, ambitions, agency, authority, assertiveness, attitudes, and mindsets. When you stand in your power, you are conscious of the demands and forces around you. As a result, you make conscious choices to raise yourself and others, and embrace this power for good.

CHAPTER 2

MINDSETS MATTER

"Mindset is everything. Your success
begins and ends with mindset. In between
it's grit that carries you through."

LEAURA ALDERSON

YOUR MINDSETS form when you are young. I was always a curious child. I liked to solve problems, work through puzzles, and invent or make things. My favorite board game was Clue, which is centered around solving a murder mystery. I like this game so much, I even named my cats after the main characters—Colonel Mustard and Professor Plum! I enjoyed playing the game because it required me to look for evidence, identify patterns, and uncover the characters' motivations. I grew up to be fascinated with people's motivations and the link between your mindsets, behaviors, and results, and how your sense of your personal power could be the X-factor for your success.

My family moved every year when I was growing up, as my father was an ambitious corporate executive. Being the new kid in class, year after year, made me stronger as I became increasingly comfortable to start over, again and again. Each year, I would return to school in a new grade, in a new house, and in a new town. Eventually, I began to enjoy the process of reinventing myself each summer. In short, my mindset completely changed—which had a huge impact on my ability to embrace all the new settings I found myself in.

Later in life, I became interested in mindsets. Specifically, how mindsets affect your sense of satisfaction and productivity, as well as how a mismatch in your mindsets and your work culture can become demoralizing and lead to a sense of personal powerlessness. Always curious, I embarked on a research study about how female leaders design and manage their careers. I found three archetypes that explain how women make career decisions and what kind of support they need as they build their careers in challenging times. This research led to the framework I call *Accelerate You!* Mindsets matter hugely to your success. Do you know your mindsets? Are your mindsets holding you back from achieving what you want?

In this chapter, you will learn the importance of mindsets. You will see that your mindsets are flexible, changeable, and can either accelerate you forward toward your goals and dreams or limit you by becoming a barrier to your success. When your mindsets are aligned with your role in life or in the workplace, and match your workplace culture, you will feel inspired, productive, and satisfied. Your mindsets can be measured, helping you adjust them if necessary. By understanding why mindsets matter, and how they work, you'll be able to make better decisions to manage your life, career, and business.

What are mindsets?

Mindsets are your established patterns of thought, or a set of preferred attitudes or motivations. These mindsets frame your thinking and how you make sense or meaning of the world around you. Mindsets drive your habits, behaviors, and outcomes. They influence how you think, feel, and react in any given situation. While you have your default mindsets, you can change your mindsets, and this can impact whether you succeed or fail.

Examples of mindsets are your beliefs, values, determination, hope, humility, gratitude, patience, feeling of purpose, and sense of connection to your personal power. Mindsets relate to how you approach problems and set goals, how you communicate, and how you take on or share responsibility with others. Mindsets drive collaboration, creativity, and innovation. Mindsets even determine your relationship to change and how you can lead and manage change when collaborating with others. Researchers have found that different mindsets are required for different situations, such as creating something new, starting up a business, or scaling a business. A research team I led found that women draw on different mindsets to orienteer the different pivots in their careers and businesses. You will learn more about these mindsets and patterns of career management later in this chapter.

As humans, we are bombarded with information every second of the day and we have developed the ability to sift through the information using our internal sensory circuits (for example, sight, touch, hearing, smell, and taste) to bring information to the nervous system throughout the body and the brain where information, memories, and emotions are stored. You access and retrieve this information in different parts of your brain and body through an intricate superhighway of neural pathways. Humans use mental cues, filters, or shortcuts to make decisions consciously and unconsciously using these systems of neural pathways. Researchers refer to these mental shortcuts as meta programs. Think of these meta programs as your unique software that operates your internal systems. Meta programs are cognitive and behavioral attitudes, motivations, styles, or patterns that influence your decisions, behaviors, or interactions with the world.

According to research conducted by Stanford psychologist Carol Dweck, PhD, your mindset can determine your relationship with achievement and success. She found that there are two types of mindsets: a fixed mindset and a growth mindset. If you have a fixed mindset, you believe that your abilities are fixed and unchangeable—and that you either have the talent, capability, or intelligence to succeed or you don't. If you have a fixed mindset, you aren't motivated by challenge. On the contrary, you are highly resistant to change, experimentation, learning new skills or concepts, and reaching your potential. If you have a fixed mindset, it could be impacting your ability to reach your goals. Alternatively, if you have a growth mindset, you believe that you can cultivate talent, capability, and intelligence through effort and persistence, and you use challenges and experimentation to learn and grow.

Mindsets affect your wellbeing and your resilience. If you had a growth mindset as a child, you grew up curious, enjoying challenges and discovering new things. As you grew into adulthood, your growth mindset helped you to persevere with life's setbacks. In contrast, children and adults with fixed mindsets are less resilient, give up more easily, and tend to seek validation to prove their worth to others and to themselves. You can develop a growth mindset and change your relationship with success. Holly Ransom, in her book *The Leading Edge*, describes leadership as a state of mind and encourages leaders to adopt core mindsets: anchor to purpose, frame your choices, own your narrative, build your bounce, choose your attitude, and stay hungry for feedback. She talks about mindsets, methods, and mastery of leadership, and encourages you to first lead yourself by choosing your mindsets.

How can you measure and change your mindsets?

When you learn how to identify your thinking patterns, you can make changes in your mindsets to make better decisions and achieve more results faster, bringing you the consistency you are seeking in achieving your goals and finding fulfillment, happiness, and success.

Start by developing self-awareness, which is the ability to see yourself clearly and understand who you are, how others see you, and how you fit into the world. Self-awareness gives you power. Knowing your strengths and mindsets enables you to see yourself clearly, which enhances your confidence, courage, and creativity. Your strengths and mindsets come from exploring your relationship with yourself and with others. With practice, coaching, and tools, you can become aware of your internal thoughts, beliefs, emotions, motivations, mindsets, and reactions, as well as your awareness of how other people view you and your strengths, motivations, behaviors, and reactions. With this internal and external self-awareness, you can also understand situations, activities, interactions, jobs, and work cultures that make you feel empowered or discouraged.

Tasha Eurich, PhD, in a *Harvard Business Review* article titled "What Self-Awareness Really Is (and How to Cultivate It)," describes four self-awareness archetypes that illuminate how well you know yourself and how well you understand how others see you. Eurich suggests that leaders must develop both internal and external awareness. Why would you want to do this? Eurich's research found that having high internal and external awareness makes leaders more effective, promotable, and productive—leading to more profitable companies. Find the archetype that best describes you from the following grid.

The Four Self-Awareness Archetypes

	External Self-Awareness	
Internal Self-Awareness (HIGH)	**Introspector** You know yourself but don't challenge your views, gather feedback, or search your blind spots sabotaging relationships and limiting your success	**Aware** You know yourself and your goals, seek the views of others, feedback, and gain the benefit of full self-awareness
Internal Self-Awareness (LOW)	**Seeker** You don't know yourself, your values, or your personal truths, often feel stuck and frustrated with yourself and your relationships	**Pleaser** You focus on pleasing others or appearing in a certain manner rather than what you want or need. Overtime you make choices that don't support your success or fulfillment
	LOW HIGH	

What is your archetype now and how can you power up your internal and external self-awareness?

You can develop awareness of how others perceive you by working with supportive, trustworthy friends, family members, colleagues, coaches, and mentors. Seek feedback regularly from a variety of sources. Surround yourself with supportive allies. The people around you impact your behaviors, thought patterns, and how you view yourself. Choose people who will support you, inspire you, and enable you to achieve your goals as you master new capabilities and evolve. Focus on leveraging your strengths in areas where you are highly motivated to succeed. Work with a mentor or a coach who can help you identify self-awareness and understand your strengths and how to reach your goals.

Another great way to develop self-awareness is to take one of the many mindset assessments available. Mindsets have been studied and can be measured. Leadership and business management researchers have looked at the dimensions of our mindsets for decades and, as a result, define mindsets as attitudes or motivations that underpin your intentional and unintentional patterns of thinking and acting. Many of the women I work with have lost their connection to their strengths and know very little about their mindsets and, more importantly, how mindsets can make them successful.

There's a variety of online assessments that will enable you to learn more about yourself and build self-awareness about your mindsets. These online assessments offer a point-in-time snapshot that will illuminate what makes you tick. When you know yourself better, you have clarity and are more confident. When you know your mindsets and what motivates you, you can make better choices. You can select workplaces with cultures that make you happier and more productive. To accelerate yourself toward your goals, use tools that enable you to mark and measure your mindsets and dimensions of your personal power.

Fingerprint for Success (F4S) is one of the assessment tools I use when coaching leaders because it features a simple and intuitive online user interface containing a vast range of tools for individuals, teams, and organizations. This tool enables you to develop yourself, your team, and the culture in your business. Know your mindsets. Track your mindsets over time. Choose to power up your leadership and your results by making choices aligned to your mindsets and your goals. When you know your mindsets, you can change your strategies for communication, decision making, and collaboration based on different situations, objectives, and the people involved. Learn what motivates you to initiate and seize opportunities, take risks, make decisions, and solve problems. Learn your attitudes toward power and how you prefer to lead and be led. Tools like this build your self-awareness and help you build your container to hold your personal power.

Take the free *Accelerate You!* Fingerprint for Success assessment (https://app.fingerprintforsuccess.

com/sign-up/organization/join/b1310e779a2ef50
0ed3657f35481a43e/create-account) and review your
results and awaken to your strengths. This survey
will provide insight and clarity on your mindsets and
what is important to you. Knowing your strengths,
motivations, and blind spots can help you increase
your happiness and wellbeing, find meaning and
purpose, boost your performance, and increase your
capability to communicate and collaborate effectively. Developing this deep self-awareness will assist
you to leverage your strengths, power up your leadership, and accomplish goals. These tools can also
help you connect to your personal power and manage your stress, energy, vitality, and health. You will
learn more about mindsets to increase your power in
the next chapter.

Mindsets and organizational culture

Michelle Duval, a researcher, pioneer in professional
coaching, and founder of Fingerprint for Success, has
been working with thousands of companies around
the world to develop leaders, high-performing teams,
and organizational cultures that support creativity,
innovation, and entrepreneurial success. In her work,
she began to see patterns emerging about the attitudes and motivations of successful startup founders,
business owners and leaders, and compared them to
leaders who had failed. As a result, she has been able

to identify the mindsets that enable success in different contexts.

By mapping the current culture or collective mindsets of the individuals in organizations, teams can self-identify areas in the organization and its culture that are aligned with their personal values and goals for the future. If organizations are seeking to better support enterprising leaders and innovation, the tools for measuring culture enable them to identify strategies for organizational development and investment.

Individuals can use the F4S tool to better understand how to select organizations with cultures that inspire productivity, engagement, and a sense of belonging, enabling them to actively manage their careers. I use this tool with my MBA students learning how to scale growth in organizations, and how individual mindsets and behaviors are required at different stages of organizational change. The F4S tool is also invaluable to help startup founders choose their co-founders and build their teams based on the culture they want to create. Understanding individual and team mindsets enables team members to be more collaborative and productive, increase effective communication, and reduce organizational conflict that naturally occurs during the creative, startup, and scaleup processes. The mindsets revealed through the F4S assessment also underpin the framework of *Accelerate You!* You will learn more about each of these mindsets in the chapters to come.

Moving between mindsets
for different objectives

After partnering with Startup Genome and researching thousands of entrepreneurs in fifty-five cities around the world, Duval found a link between founder attitudes (mindsets) and their ability to attract investment and sell their companies quickly for large returns. She was able to compare these entrepreneurial mindsets for success with the mindsets required to scale, grow, or build businesses over time. Ultimately, she found that different mindsets are required in different contexts. In this study of the global startup ecosystem, the researchers were also able to see how different ecosystems in different parts of the world display different mindsets that enable innovation, as well as startup and scaleup growth.

What can you take from Duval's research and apply to your own life? Leaders with a mindset based on big-picture thinking can influence and inspire themselves and their peers during times of change. Those leaders who can act on their vision, reference their own experience when making timely decisions, and use their intuition in solving problems can be successful in startup environments or when the situation requires them to forge a new, creative path. Alternatively, when leaders are required to innovate, scale, or grow a sound business model, they must be capable of flexing their mindsets to concentrate on business metrics and mitigate risks, which typically requires more concrete and conservative thinking.

You can develop the flexibility to move between mindsets for different objectives. With this increased flexibility and knowledge of organizational cultures, you can make better choices in your career in terms of the roles you select and the organizations you join. You are likely to be more productive, satisfied, and successful if your individual values and mindsets align with the role you are in or choose to take and with the organizational culture. Look for workplaces and organizational cultures that align with your mindsets. These organizations will provide psychological safety or environments where you will feel supported to experiment, make mistakes, and be enterprising and innovative.

As you make the connection between your core values, strengths, ambitions, attitudes (mindsets), agency, and authority, you can use your mindsets as your compass to help you design your future, navigating the powerful pivots that you will need to make to change your life, manage your career, lead a team, or start up a new project or business.

Navigators, surveyors, and pioneers

Today your career and resume are likely to look like a series of workplace opportunities you have taken that reflect your evolving and varied interests and abilities. Gone are the days where you "set and forget" your career. Life and workplaces are filled with disruptions—downsizing, reorganizations, and closures. Many people combine multiple part-time roles to give them the flexibility and diversity they're seeking, and some have a startup project on the side. Increasingly, startups are a great source of employment and experience.

Learning to manage your career is an essential skill that requires you to continually pivot and reinvent yourself, which will call you to develop and manage your mindsets and capabilities to bridge the many transitions in your life, career, and business.

My research with Tania Machet, PhD, and Michelle Duval has focused on how women in the tech sector manage their careers and businesses. We've also used Fingerprint for Success to learn more about how women make decisions across their careers. We studied female leaders at various career stages in the tech industry and found they have three styles in orienteering their careers and businesses based on their preferences for change and challenge. This research involved a process of appreciative inquiry where individuals were asked to explain where they were and where they aspired to be in the future.

The women in this study shared their values, dreams, aspirations, trade-offs, and disappointments. They described how they designed their careers, started up their companies, built their teams, and commercialized their research. They described the barriers they face, and what they need to support their leadership and advancement. They also described the gaps they were experiencing both within themselves and within the work systems in which they were employed.

With my research team, we identified three core mindsets used by these career and venture "change artists." Our work built upon the work of Michelle Gibbings, outlined in her book *Career Leap*. We found three career decision-making profiles: navigators, surveyors, and pioneers. Here's a brief overview:

- **Navigators** prefer clear, well-articulated career ladders or paths of progress and have a low tolerance for career or business risk. They prefer well-tested career routes and are reluctant to experiment with unknown or ill-defined pathways. They view their career strategy as a series of logical steps from one to another. Their professional roles are usually in the same division, functional area, or organization. They rarely explore different sectors or types of organizations.

- **Surveyors** have more curiosity and are motivated to disrupt themselves more often as they have a higher risk tolerance. Surveyors push boundaries and take the less established career path, and are keen to discover new roles or options they haven't previously experienced or considered. They view career leaps or pivots as "destinations" of their own design and enjoy the adventure of the career pivot.

- **Pioneers** explore career leaps or career options that few before them have tried. They aspire to create something new and are comfortable with risky, ambiguous, or non-existent career pathways. They are excited by the challenge.

I first became interested in how we navigate career change when I found myself designing my own transformational journey, which included leaving the US and coming to Australia. My transformational journey was akin to walking a spiraled path or labyrinth. I experienced the death of my marriage, which led to feelings of loss felt from a divorce, the loss felt from not achieving all that I had hoped for in my life, and a sense of isolation that came with moving from one country to another—leaving family and friends behind. I didn't know it at the time, but I later learned through my research that my life and career decision-making pattern is most like the pioneer archetype. I was willing to take big risks to make a big leap forward. Even though I was experiencing pain and loss, I knew that I could design my life from a blank canvas. I just needed time and a process to find clarity and my inspiration. I learned I needed to act and rely on my own inner wisdom.

My success required me to step into my own personal power, and appreciate and celebrate even the smallest steps forward. After rebuilding my life and career in a new country, the pandemic forced me to face loss once more and brought emotions like anger, isolation, and grief. I needed to clear these negative emotions and beliefs before I could regenerate myself and design my next steps. These types of changes can leave you feeling a loss of purpose and not knowing which way to turn next. My coach helped me find my "North star" and chart my future to success on my terms. I have transformed my sense of loss and now coach others to create beautiful and successful lives, careers, and ventures. As a mindset researcher and a coach, I work with my clients to enable them to find their own North star.

Leveling up in your life, career, or business can feel like riding a roller coaster, so it helps to have a map to guide you through traveled terrain. You can empower yourself by understanding that your decision-making pattern may be based on how much risk or change you want to take on at different stages in your life or career. It is also helpful to remember that your decision-making style, like so many things, can change over time.

In this book, you are learning about the five mindsets required to be a change agent in your life, career, or business. These mindsets are *clarity, confidence, courage, creativity, and the ability to embrace and embody change.* In Chapter 1, you discovered a series of questions—related to these five mindsets—which you can ask yourself to determine whether you're leaking your power. You can develop these mindsets and other capabilities to make the pivots that will close any power gaps you may have. In the chapters that follow, you will learn more about assessing power gaps, closing the gaps by building flexibility in your mindsets, and how to make the power pivots you choose based on your specific goals and context.

CHAPTER 3

ASSESS AND ADDRESS YOUR POWER GAPS

"I'm finally ready to own my own power, to say,
'This is who I am.' If you like it, you like it. And if you
don't like it, you don't. So, watch out; I'm gonna fly."

OPRAH WINFREY

HAVE EXPERIENCED all five power gaps that
affect both men and women. I have written this
book for women because I want women to have the
support they need to discover their hidden strengths
and to gain clarity on what motivates and inspires
them. The key to powering up your leadership is
leveraging your inspiration, intuition, and imagination, while being able to initiate change that creates
impact. To accelerate yourself forward, you must
close the five power gaps and adopt or strengthen five
important mindsets. This process is an "inside job."

The journey toward transformation is one of self-discovery, self-awareness, and self-management. It is a process of learning by doing.

There have been times in my life, career, and in business when fear held me back. My fear blocked my vision for what was possible and blocked my path to opportunities that were open to me. I was frozen in place, driven by my perfectionism and my fear of being found to be an imposter. What did that look like for me? I overperformed instead of identifying priorities and setting boundaries. Eventually, I learned to give up the false security that comes with endless to-do lists. I began to say "no" to unrealistic deadlines, and "yes" to roles with more reasonable workloads. I left roles that were no longer challenging, or where I was being bullied or not respected. This required me to confidently assert my needs, communicate from a place of strength, and disrupt myself and change jobs if required. These power strategies were lessons learned after many missteps and missed opportunities.

Slowly, I began to recognize and awaken to my strengths and to look at the big picture—what was possible and what would inspire me. I developed an action plan instead of hiding out or staying frozen with fear. I began to advocate for myself. I became comfortable with making decisions, describing my contributions, and influencing others. I routinely assessed how far I had come, experimenting with new mindsets and skills. When I found solutions that worked and were sustainable, I felt my personal power rise. This journey at times felt isolating, but I learned to reach out and surround myself with a supportive community of peers, allies, mentors, coaches, and career sponsors. By increasing my self-awareness, asking for feedback, and embodying new mindsets and strategies, I was able to make powerful pivots toward my dreams.

In this chapter, you will discover how harmful gaps in your personal power can affect your life, career, and business. You will learn how to identify a power gap and understand how the gaps form and grow over time. You will be able to assess your own personal power that may have formed over time. Most importantly, you will learn how to close your power gaps so that you can accelerate forward toward your goals.

What are power gaps and why do they happen?

When you are connected to your personal power, your default state of mind is linked to and leveraging your strengths—your abilities, ambitions, accomplishments, attitudes, agency, and authority to give you consciousness and clarity. With clarity, you unlock the connection to your confidence, courage, creativity, and the ability to embrace, lead, and celebrate the change you are creating in the world. You have access to this power every moment. When you experience a lack of clarity on how you want to leverage your strengths to solve the challenges you face, you are experiencing a personal power gap. When you don't feel connected to your confidence, courage, or creativity, you are experiencing a power gap. When you don't feel connected to your motivations and resources to create the change you desire, you are experiencing a power gap.

No one feels powerful every moment of the day. It's natural to have thoughts, emotions, or experiences that pull you out of your power, causing a gap in your power supply or a break in the connection to your power, which creates a power gap. Moment-to-moment feelings, thoughts, urges, memories, and motivations are operating either consciously or unconsciously in your mind to drive your behaviors and decision making.

If your goal is to power up your leadership, you'll need to tap into your unconscious mind to unlock important internal resources that can accelerate you toward your goals or, in contrast, pull you away or out of your power—creating a power gap. To power up, you are committing to become a more conscious leader by boosting your awareness of the conscious and unconscious aspects of yourself that affect your thoughts and behavior.

Human brains are hardwired to act instinctively in ways to keep you safe, sending you into fight, flight, or freeze states. When the opportunity in front of you is so big it scares you, and you hear yourself saying, "I can't do that!," you may have slipped into an unconscious mindset to protect yourself. If you don't consciously connect with your personal power to bring clarity and the confidence to move forward despite your fear, you could unconsciously sabotage yourself with the words you use to describe yourself, or the messages you tell yourself.

If you continue in this state of mind, you are abandoning your personal power supply. When you watch yourself struggle with a decision, run away from opportunities that align with your vision of success, or freeze in a particular situation, you can intentionally power up your leadership by assessing and closing these power gaps. Becoming conscious and self-aware is one of many strategies to identify and close your power gaps. Stephen R. Covey, in his book, *The 7 Habits of Highly Effective People*, states, "Power is the faculty or capacity to act, the strengths and potency to accomplish something. It is the vital energy to make choices and decisions. It also includes the capacity to overcome deeply embedded habits and to cultivate higher, more effective ones."

How do you assess a power gap and why is it important?

You can assess your power gaps by becoming conscious of your unconscious habits and states of mind. You experience your personal power through your senses and their interpretations of your thoughts, emotions, behaviors, and levels of energy. You experience your power when you are connected to your internal resources, and you are aware and managing your thoughts, emotions, and behaviors to achieve your goals. You can experience your power by assessing your level of energy, as well as your levels of clarity, confidence, courage, and creativity, and your readiness to lead, embrace, embody, and celebrate change.

If you are feeling a lack of clarity, confidence, courage, or creativity, or you are uncomfortable with the changes around you, or how you are leading the change in your life, career, or business, you may be experiencing a power gap. If you have felt powerful one moment and then in the next moment you lack confidence or are paralyzed with fear, you are experiencing a power gap. If you are procrastinating, getting inconsistent results, or not satisfied with your movement or momentum toward your goals, you are probably experiencing a power gap in some area of your life. If you feel burnt out, disillusioned, hopeless, or just unhappy, you may be experiencing a power gap that you can close by making different choices.

Instead of blaming yourself, or feeling shame or guilt, you can learn to assess and close your power gap. Having this skill will boost your resilience and wellbeing as well as your confidence. The key to consistent results and progress toward your goals is to learn what it feels like to be out of your power, to know what pulls you out of your power zone, and how you can quickly close your power gaps.

Here are some examples of power gaps:

- Staying in the wrong job, wrong relationship, or with the wrong strategy for too long.

- Being paralyzed by fear, imposter syndrome, or perfectionism, and therefore not creating the future you desire.

- Failing to identify and pursue the challenges that will inspire and strengthen you, failing to ask for what you need, or failing to build the boundaries you need to focus on your goals.

- Hiding out, failing to step forward, or not speaking up to express your ideas, your personal truths, or your needs or wants.

- Not connecting with mentors, sponsors, allies, or your support team to achieve your goals.

Power gaps can happen in a moment, or they can build over time. Let's explore the difference in the next two sections.

How do power gaps happen in the moment?

Inside your brain, something known as the amygdala can trigger your fight, flight, or freeze responses to physical, social, and emotional threats. The amygdala regulates your feelings of fear, anxiety, and aggression. When the amygdala is triggered by something in the environment, a memory, or a negative thought or emotion, it flips a switch to disrupt your prefrontal cortex (where you do most of your rational thinking) so that your emotions dominate your thinking and diminish your ability to self-regulate your behavior. This process was described by Daniel Goleman, the father of emotional intelligence research, as an "amygdala hijack." When you are triggered or hijacked, your brain stops comprehending, planning, deciding, and learning.

Neuroscientists Matthew Lieberman and Naomi Eisenberger have found that your emotional responses to psychological pain (for example, pain from being rejected, treated unfairly, punished, and so on) use the same neural circuits in your brain that are used when you have physical injuries. They found that the brain treats abstract social experiences like jealousy and justice in the same way as it treats pain and pleasure. When you have a power gap, something happens emotionally and physically to hijack your mental state. You experience a thought, an emotional response, or a trigger that launches you into a physical and mental reaction, unleashing your worst insecurities and causing you to think that someone's actions or behaviors are signs that you are not respected, not enough, or don't matter. Your mind and body are overwhelmed with your reaction, and you may not even be conscious of the hijacking.

Brain scientists have discovered the body-mind mechanics behind these hijackings and are providing us with more tools to prevent or recover from these hijacked moments in which you have been kicked out of your power zone. In these moments, you are leaking your power as you simultaneously move on to your next email, phone call, or meeting, or go home to your family. This hijacking can lead to any number of problem behaviors that you may develop to avoid the pain of experiencing these insecurities or self-doubt.

Examples of these behaviors include reacting defensively in the heat of the moment, beginning to micromanage, developing a tendency to overwork, shying away from opportunities, procrastinating, devolving into a cycle of blame or shame, or numbing yourself with food, drink, or social media to compensate for, or distract yourself from, the pain of your perceptions or misperceptions. Most people were not raised to be aware of how their minds and bodies work together and must actively reset their mind-body connection. These moments that hijack you can happen anywhere and are often unavoidable because of your past experiences, including how you were raised and how you learned about your personal power, and because of the daily situations you face.

These hijacking moments can be triggered by your work culture. In an article published by *MIT Sloan Management Review*, titled "Why Every Leader Needs to Worry About Toxic Culture," researchers identified workplace attributes that limit your sense of psychological safety or personal belonging. These attributes of toxicity are:

- Disrespect,
- Non-inclusion,
- Unethical and dishonest behavior,
- Lack of regulatory compliance,
- Dysfunctional competition, and
- Bullying, harassment, and hostility.

These toxic attributes can make you emotionally and physically sick from the constant hijackings they create within you. If you aren't aware of them, you may be losing or leaking your personal power from the constant triggering and internalizing your emotional and physical reactions as your fault or avoidable (when they are neither).

Ruchika Tulshyan and Jodi-Ann Burey, authors of a *Harvard Business Review* article titled "Stop Telling Women They Have Imposter Syndrome," have conducted research on the impact of systemic bias and exclusion, and how it creates in women feelings that have traditionally been described as imposter syndrome when women doubt their abilities. This diagnosis has traditionally not considered the effects of racism, classism, xenophobia, ageism, or other biases against women. We will discuss imposter syndrome in the following chapters.

How do you lose your personal power over time?

Chapters 5 through 9 will give you a framework for recognizing how you may get derailed and lose your power, and how you can pivot to get back into your personal power zone. You can let your personal power drain away by holding on to limiting or negative beliefs, emotions, or influences that become filters that block you, distract you, slow your momentum, and keep you feeling stuck. These negative thought patterns can form the basis of how you view yourself, opportunities, and the strategies you use to achieve your goals. How you assess yourself is pivotal to your future growth and goal achievement.

To discover these negative thought patterns, develop self-awareness of when they are with you and how they limit you. These are stories you tell about yourself and your capabilities that limit you. For example, when you think or say, "I am not ready," or "I am not smart enough," you are sabotaging yourself and leaking your power. Begin to question these stories, bust these personal myths, and rewrite your options. Notice when you procrastinate. Unearth the rules or limits that you put in place to guide your decision making, or the times you find it difficult to make decisions or set priorities or boundaries. Are there circumstances that trigger you, limiting your decision-making abilities or your ability to use your personal power or voice to influence others? Notice the situations and contexts when you have internal conflicts and confusions. These moments are examples of instances when you are leaking power.

Get curious about what causes these triggers, negative patterns, or behaviors. Learn how to recognize them, including what causes them, and how you can interrupt your default patterns. Perhaps you're aware of an "inner critic" stealing your confidence, but you may be unaware of other problematic patterns that drain your power, including performance anxiety, chronic overworking, burnout, people pleasing, perfectionism, approval seeking, and imposter syndrome. Which of these behaviors have you noticed in yourself? These patterns can drain your power and slow your momentum toward your goals. If you are ready to accelerate yourself forward, start with self-awareness. Learn to identify these patterns and how to interrupt them, and even how to clear the pattern from your repertoire. You can learn new strategies to be more resourceful and to close your power gaps. Working with a mentor or coach can be helpful to develop your internal and external awareness so you can make choices to disrupt your negative patterns and clear what is leaking your power.

You can lose your power over time if you are not aware of your behaviors and emotions, or if you are not practiced in recognizing, naming, and managing your emotions. Your emotions are signposts that can help you get to your intended destination or to make a powerful pivot. Emotions provide you with important information. Learn to read them. Many women have been told all their life, "You are too emotional," or "Never show your anger; it isn't ladylike." Our parents and grandparents typically came from cultures and generations that didn't talk about emotions or, if emotions were discussed, we were taught to deny or suppress them. Over the years, many women, thinking it was a strategy for success, have denied and bottled up their emotions to fit into a male-dominated workplace.

Thankfully, our workplaces and definitions of effective leadership are changing. Recognizing and managing your emotions, and recognizing the emotions of others, are part of your success formula. For example, when you are feeling rage, instead of bottling your emotions, you could ask yourself, "Can I look deeper?" You may find that your anger is there because you feel voiceless. As you go deeper, you may become clear on what you want instead of feeling voiceless. This could be an opportunity for you to explore and express what you want and need. Create the space to recognize yourself and listen to yourself. In our workplaces, we also need to acknowledge that we are emotional beings and ask ourselves, "How does our leadership and culture support everyone to be seen and heard, and how can we build our capacity and support our collective emotional agility?"

Researchers combining neuroscience, engineering, computer science, and psychology are developing ways to detect, recognize, and measure your emotions. Your emotions can be measured by their energetic vibration or frequencies and can be ranked or sequenced from their highest vibrations or frequency to the lowest. For example, the top emotion with the highest frequency, joy, is followed by happiness, optimism, hopefulness, contentment, and courage. Moving down the list are emotions like boredom, pessimism, impatience, disappointment, worry, blame, anger, fear, apathy, guilt, and shame, with each emotion moving lower in frequency toward powerlessness. Scientists measure these emotions and continue to add to our knowledge of the spectrum of emotions and their effect on our internal mental states, behavior patterns, and intended outcomes. Emotions with higher frequencies can increase your personal power. When you develop personal strategies to experience higher frequency emotions, you begin to reset or increase your personal power supply. We'll discuss this in more detail in Chapter 4.

Alicia Nortje, PhD, has analyzed and reviewed the tools that can be used to assess your emotional intelligences and develop your emotional quotient (EQ). These emotional intelligences are capabilities that support your leadership and management, and help you be self-aware and manage yourself in a variety of situations. There are dimensions to emotional intelligence that you can begin to explore and develop:

- **Emotional self-awareness** (your ease in expressing feelings).

- **Assertiveness** (your comfort to assert your needs or say "yes" or "no" when you want).

- **Independence** (your preference to lead or follow).

- **Empathy** (your sensitivity to the feelings of others).

- **Adaptability** (your preferences in problem solving, reality testing, and flexibility).

- **Stress management** (your capability to manage stress and your impulses).

If you want to build your internal awareness and capacity to lead and create the change you want in your life, career, and business, it's crucial that you get to know your emotions and develop your EQ. We'll discuss this in more detail in later chapters.

Finding your power gaps

As I've explained, in my work with female leaders, they report feeling a lack of clarity, confidence, courage, or creativity, or a lack of understanding of how to create the change they are seeking.

These women are describing power gaps that are common for women of all ages, education levels, professions, industries, and roles—from students to entrepreneurs to corporate leaders. These power gaps are often associated with a lack of energy, inspiration, hope, positivity, self-trust, and self-authority, which decreases your capacity for self-worth, connection, and collaboration.

As a quick recap, the five damaging power gaps that you might experience are:

1 Not recognizing your strengths (accomplishments, ambitions, abilities, agency, attitudes, assertiveness, and authority) and a sense of your value and impact.

2 Letting your fear hold you back from acting or communicating with strength.

3 Failing to back yourself or to ask for what you require or deserve.

4 Being uncomfortable making decisions, solving problems, setting goals, or using or developing your resources.

5 Disconnecting from your strengths or isolating from influential support.

Take a moment to answer the following questions and assess if you have any of these power gaps. If you do, this book will help you learn how to close them. If you are experiencing a number of these power gaps, and experiencing them often, this is an indication that you should focus on your personal leadership development in these key areas. Consider what these gaps are costing you and how they might be blocking your path or slowing you down from achieving more results faster. Identify which gap or gaps are most important for you to close and work on closing them first. In Chapters 5 through 9, we will explore more deeply the mindsets you can develop to close your gaps.

FINDING YOUR POWER GAPS

POWER GAP	DO YOU EXPERIENCE THIS POWER GAP?	IF "YES," HOW OFTEN DO YOU EXPERIENCE THE GAP?
Not recognizing your strengths, and a sense of your value and impact	Yes No	Often Sometimes Rarely
Letting your fear hold you back from acting or communicating with strength	Yes No	Often Sometimes Rarely
Failing to back yourself or to ask for what you require or deserve	Yes No	Often Sometimes Rarely
Being uncomfortable making decisions, solving problems, setting goals, or using or developing your resources	Yes No	Often Sometimes Rarely
Disconnecting from your strengths or isolating from influential support	Yes No	Often Sometimes Rarely

Are you experiencing any of these gaps? If you answered "yes," know that it is not your fault, and you are not flawed. What you need is a pathway and process in your immediate control to manage your personal power and to make wise choices for yourself and others.

Developing a plan to close your power gaps

You can develop a plan to close your power gaps by answering the following questions:

1   Which power gaps are you experiencing? In what contexts? What is triggering or contributing to the gap?

2   How do these power gaps impact your ability to lead on a regular basis?

3   What are some of the ways these power gaps negatively affect your life, career, and business? How are these gaps stopping you from achieving what you desire?

4   What would you be able to do or gain if you closed these power gaps?

5   What is the most important gap you can close today that will create the change and the future you desire?

Once you have the answers to these questions, you can begin to identify your priorities and where you want to begin the process of internal transformation. If the answers to your questions are within your control, you can close your personal power gaps and build your personal power reserve by amplifying your capabilities, shifting your mindsets, and adjusting personal behaviors that support your goals, which is the focus of this book.

Stepping into a new sense of personal power means having self-awareness and the courage to untangle a web of circumstances, relationships, and self-limitations (negative beliefs, emotions, patterns, and influences) that keep you from radiating your true self and capabilities. Closing your power gap requires you to want to make change and to take responsibility for your growth. It requires you to own your personal power.

When some people think about making a change, their emotions take over, fears arise, and memories come up about the last time they attempted to make a change. In short, your thought patterns and commitment to change can be hijacked. In these moments, you feel your inspiration, intention, commitment, and power drain away. Part of the change process is decluttering or clearing your mind of these memories, emotions, patterns, or influences, and minimizing the effects of these triggers that derail your focus and intention. Pippa Grange, PhD, through her work with world-class athletes, studied fear and how it brings on anxiety, shame, and a need for perfectionism. In her book, *Fear Less: How to Win Your Way in Work and Life*, she illustrates how focusing on your passion and opening yourself to what makes you vulnerable can help you release your fears and lead to a more satisfying pathway to success. Releasing your fear by backing yourself and your dreams is what modern leaders call wholehearted leadership.

Once you have identified your power gaps and what these gaps are costing you, you can make a choice to close the gaps. Making the choice to find the mindsets and behaviors to strengthen your personal power leads you to a more authentic leadership style, which is unique to you. It is possible to identify and close your power gaps, and pivot toward joy, happiness, and success. The process of closing a power gap is called making a **power pivot**, which is the focus of Chapter 4.

CHAPTER 4

MAKE YOUR POWER PIVOTS

"Freeing yourself was one thing; claiming
ownership of that freed self was another."

TONI MORRISON

One of the most valuable things you can learn
is when to make a power pivot. A pivot is a shift,
adjustment, or change in course or direction.
These pivots can include changing your mindsets,
taking a new step forward, or shifting your strategy
toward success. Often before you change directions
in your career, business, or in life—when you let go
of values, beliefs, attitudes, or behaviors that no longer serve you—it can feel unsettling, uncomfortable,
or even painful. Instead of avoiding these moments,
understand that this is an indication it is time to
make a powerful pivot.

It's also important to note that one pivot may lead to another pivot—even if you don't know it from the outset. When I came to Australia, I was recruited for a role at the University of Technology Sydney. I was excited about the opportunity to make a big pivot in my life; to redefine what success meant to me and how I wanted to create a positive impact in the world. However, as time passed, I realized the role that brought me to Australia was no longer challenging me. I lost motivation, which made me question my sense of purpose and direction. I could feel my energy draining from me.

I realized it was time for another series of pivots. I sought out more challenging roles, first expanding the job description of my current job to increase my sense of inspiration and contribution. I began mentoring female leaders and startup founders. I completed further education and training that fascinated me and prepared me for the roles and pivots I wanted to make in the future. Over the years, I pivoted into roles that were in line with my passions and new vision for myself and offered me the challenges I needed to keep me inspired. I learned to recognize when it was time to make a change, to move out of my comfort zone, and to tweak my mindsets. In short, I became exceptionally good at raising my personal power.

In this chapter, you will learn how to raise your personal power by changing or tweaking your mindsets. You will discover the five mindsets that can power up your leadership, life, career, and business management.

How can you raise your power?

The journey to power up your leadership is a heroine's journey to identify and close your power gaps and raise your personal power. You raise your personal power by recognizing your strengths, and letting go of fear or other emotions that hold you back. You raise your personal power when you make the choice to establish a boundary, prioritize yourself, or leave a context that is not supporting you. You raise your personal power when you activate the mindset that will raise your energy and ability to advocate for yourself—amplifying your voice and actions to embrace, embody, and lead the change you want to see in the world.

When you identify and fully experience your emotions, you can hold the space for your emotions to move through you. If you uncover emotions that are "stuck," you can clear them and intentionally move yourself to emotions with higher vibrations. It is important to give yourself permission to feel every emotion—recognizing each one and following its arc, and then taking it one step further to shift your emotional mood. With practice, you can raise your emotions to higher frequencies and take responsibility for your internal states. Shifting your emotions is a power pivot!

Brené Brown, PhD, has been researching emotions, and the link between organizational culture and leadership models, for decades. In her books *Daring Greatly* and *Dare to Lead*, she focuses on those moments when you feel vulnerable and more susceptible to emotions and identifies courage-building skills that make up brave leadership. Risk, uncertainty, and the threat of failure can be triggering when organizational cultures do not provide the psychological safety to be creative, enterprising, or innovative. Brown has developed tools to help you shift into more resourceful and powerful leadership practices. In another of her books, *Atlas of the Heart*, she defines eighty-seven emotions and provides an actionable framework for closing your power gaps. Her books are designed to help you identify and name your emotions, which is a literacy you may not have learned growing up.

Here are some strategies you can use to ride the waves of your emotions and raise your power.

1   **Begin to identify and embody your emotional states.** Reflect on how you are feeling. Name the emotion. Ask yourself: is the emotion bringing you positive energy, is it a resource in that moment, or is it draining your power to act resourcefully. Learn what it feels like to tap into your internal resources (experience, knowledge, technical skills, perceptions, attitudes, motivations, insights, and so on) and to experience yourself as a resourceful leader at your peak personal power. Begin to experience through your emotions when you are feeling clarity, confidence, courage, and creativity, and being an agent of positive change.

2 **Shift your mental state.** For example, if you are feeling overwhelmed, you can choose to disrupt your thinking pattern by shifting to a state of calmness and then moving your mindset to hopefulness or another positive emotion. Look deep into the feeling of overwhelm and understand the emotions that make up that feeling. You may discover you are feeling exhausted, burnt out, anxious, irritable, or angry. You may find that you are feeling afraid, guilty, or shameful. Looking even deeper, you may be feeling excited and euphoric. I have learned with my clients that you must make several small emotional pivots to move your mindset in a more positive direction. For instance, if you feel shame, it is difficult to quickly shift your mindset to joy. You must experiment to find effective strategies, which could include knowing your emotional triggers, anchoring positive emotions, using positive affirmations, practicing gratitude, engaging in activities that raise your emotions (movement, playfulness, meditation), cognitive behavioral therapies, neuro linguistic programming, and a variety of self-coaching or professional coaching practices.

3 **Monitor your progress.** Keep track of your triggers and the strategies that work and note your progress over time to pivot back into a more powerful mindset. Celebrate each step toward your positive state. Over time, you will develop your own

personal power toolkit to move yourself into your power zone.

Melanie Dean, PhD, describes personal power, including recognizing and managing its flow, and closing power gaps, in terms of managing energy. Dean brings together evidence from neurobiology, neurochemistry, biology, and physics to describe scientific ways in which you can focus your intentions and raise and hold your personal power. In her book *The Hidden Power of Emotions*, she shares a process for powering up, which includes self-awareness, building connections to your emotions, and developing your personal emotional GPS system by understanding that your emotions can increase your decision-making power and connection to your levels of personal energy.

Through the research I have conducted, and through my work with leaders, I have seen Dean's strategies in action. Indeed, I have seen that you can develop self-awareness of your levels of energy or personal power. With this awareness, you can interrupt problematic patterns by connecting with your senses and assessing your levels of clarity, confidence, courage, creativity, and readiness for change. In turn, you can shift your motivations to embody the change you want to create. Developing your emotional GPS system—and using it—is essential to develop the capabilities of a modern leader.

Here are some examples of emotions that can become your barometer. Using your senses, you can begin to perceive a rise in your personal power through observation and experimentation. Have you experienced any of the following?

- Energy and commitment rise with your playfulness, enthusiasm, inspiration, or belief in your ideas or your purpose in life.

- Concentration, focus, and clarity increase when you engage in tasks you enjoy or contexts that are aligned with your highest motivations, or when you eliminate distractions.

- A strong sense of knowing, intuition, or courage arises when you listen to your internal wisdom or trust your gut in making decisions.

- Imagination, creativity, and a sense of possibility arise when you are fearless, or acting from your strength, or in your "flow" state.

- You feel a "high" when you have taken radical action toward something you really want or a "rush" when you have been challenged and have succeeded.

These positive states of mind can be anchored and can bring you flexibility and more resources to power up and achieve your goals.

Five mindsets that enable personal power

There are five mindsets that enable personal power that are essential for leaders. These mindsets have accompanying motivations and behaviors that you can focus on to power up your leadership and close your power gaps.

MINDSETS THAT ENABLE PERSONAL POWER

MINDSET	YOUR FOCUS, MOTIVATIONS AND BEHAVIORS	YOUR STATE OF MIND
The power to see the big picture	See and communicate your vision for what is next	Clear *Inspired*
The power to initiate	Turn ideas into action Think on your feet Seize opportunities Start projects and initiatives	Confident *Impossible to possible*
The power of internal reference	Use your own criteria to make decisions Trust your gut	Courageous *Intuition*
The power of knowing and managing your personal power	Take charge Make decisions easily Comfort with your authority Influence others Control/delegate resources	Creative *Imagination and innovation*
The power of embracing, leading, and celebrating change	Understand, create, manage, and embody change Measure and celebrate change Value difference Describe impact and value propositions	Change and personal growth *Impact*

Mindsets can be strengths, or they can be your biggest weakness. It is essential that you assess and know your mindsets. The process of learning, making changes in your personal or professional life, or leading change in your career or business requires you to be aware of your mindsets and the information coming in through your senses that affect your state of mind, trigger negative memories, or affect your thinking or behavior. Once you begin to be present to these internal processes, which are linked to the process of change, you can get to the source of what might be limiting you and blocking your personal power. When you are self-aware, you can choose what you would like to change to help you accelerate toward your goal.

Changing your mindsets to accelerate your results

When you know what motivates you, and you are aware of your strengths and internal resources, you can leverage these motivations intentionally to visualize your success, make better choices, innovate, create, and achieve results faster and with less effort. Different situations require different mindsets. Successful leaders build flexibility and can adapt their mindsets for the situation. If you know your mindsets and the mindsets of those around you that you want to influence, you can adapt your approaches to accommodate their thinking patterns, develop shared goals, and influence both your behavior and theirs.

When you're more aware of your thoughts and behaviors, and you know what motivates you and how to sustain high levels of self-motivation, you are raising and sustaining your personal power and using your "genius flow" to accelerate yourself ahead. In this state, you have aligned your mindset, motivations, personal resources, masteries, and methods of operating in the world to achieve your goals. The process of entering your flow state is within your grasp and you can activate it to accelerate yourself toward your objectives.

Creating the mindset to enable this flow state is essential to your individual and group success. For example, you can use the knowledge of your preferred mindsets and motivations to maximize your energy, and to create and maintain a flow state or power state more often and for longer. When your work roles, work setting, and work culture are in alignment with your most motivating mindsets, you're more likely to feel productive, satisfied, engaged, and happy.

Carol Dweck, PhD, in her book *Mindset: Changing the Way You Think to Fulfil Your Potential*, argues that you can change a fixed mindset by focusing on the challenge, the journey, or the process, and its value in terms of learning and growth, instead of exclusively focusing on the results. She states that when you are struggling with a task or outcome, remind yourself that you are on a journey, and you haven't mastered the task *yet*. Changing your internal thought patterns, eliminating negative thoughts, and carefully choosing the language you use to describe your journey will increase your connection to your potential. Dweck also encourages you to change your mindset/s by purposefully embracing challenges.

It takes experimentation, practice, and knowledge to shift your mindsets. With practice, you will be able to identify personal power gaps, choose the mindset you need to close each power gap, and develop your own toolkit with strategies to shift your mindset. Here are some ideas to develop your toolkit, which will help you pivot into your personal power zone.

Power gap #1
Power gap: Not recognizing your strengths.

Mindsets to close this power gap:

- **Having clarity.** In this context, this means pinpointing what you want in life. With a clear vision and clarity, you can accomplish more than you ever thought possible.

How do you do this?

- Write out what would make your perfect day, week, and year. Consider what is important to you in all areas of your life, such as career and business, finances, health, friends and family, relationships, personal growth, fun and recreation, and your physical environment.

- Understand why you want this. For example, why do you want a promotion or a new job? Why do you want to take your income to the next level? Why do you want to start a new business?

- Focus on getting clear on what you want and what you *don't* want. Getting clear on what you want in your future enables you to set priorities, move toward your desires, and say "no" to things you don't want.

- **Seeing the bigger picture**. Sometimes, it's hard to see the forest for the trees. Being able to see the big picture will help you get clear on, and remain committed to, your ambition or aspirations.

How do you do this?

- Take the Fingerprint for Success assessment mentioned earlier and learn your preferences for gathering information or imagining the future.

- Big-picture thinkers inspire themselves and others by seeing the world with a broad perspective. They don't get bogged down by the details or what makes the idea difficult to implement.

- This broader view is essential in clear communication, leadership, selling, marketing, and any time you need to make your point effectively.

- **Being inspired.** When you're inspired, it feels good and powers your energy upward, creating a positive mood, giving you something to aspire toward, and encouraging you to take action.

How do you do this?

- You create inspiration when you make a decision. This process can release tension in your body and raise your energy.

- Connect with your values. Making this connection provides a valuable jumping-off point aligned with your thoughts, emotions, and motivations, which accelerates you forward.

- Reward yourself when you reach a milestone or goal. This will help maintain your focus, energy, and motivation.

Power gap #2

Power gap: Letting fear hold you back from acting or communicating with strength.

Mindsets to close this power gap:

- **Acting and communicating with strength.** Understand when fear holds you back (in which situations, with whom, and why).

How do you do this?

- Are you stressed, frightened because of a threat (real or perceived), trying to avoid something painful, or not "ready?" Your body might be having a natural response to the situation and your reaction is occurring as part of your body's sympathetic nervous systems response (called fight, flight, freeze, fawn).

- Don't assume you will be met with a negative experience or response to your actions or communications.

- Find your formula. Express what you want before you talk about what you don't want. Articulate what you want the other party to know, and involve them by asking them to help you solve the problem at hand or take the next step.

- **Harnessing the power to initiate.** This refers to your motivation to turn your ideas into action and get projects, conversations, or tasks started.

How do you do this?

- Take the Fingerprint for Success assessment and learn your preferences for initiating.

- Look for a pattern. Are there tasks, projects, or conversations that you initiate more quickly than others? How long does it take you to initiate something? How can you initiate more often or reduce the time between identifying an idea or goal and initiating action toward it?

- While you are tracking, understand if there are some areas of your life, career, or business that would benefit from you being more reflective and patient.

- **Having confidence.** This means having trust in your abilities, qualities, judgments, and the belief that you can meet the challenge in front of you.

How do you do this?

- Observe and understand what self-confidence feels like for you. Take a day or week to record all the ways you are confident and how that confidence feels in your body.

- Ask yourself, "How will I know when I have reached a satisfactory level of self-confidence?" This could inspire you to speak up more in meetings, take on a new assignment, or ask for a promotion. The answer to this question will be different for everybody. You may be surprised at your current level of self-confidence.

- Is your assessment of your self-confidence stemming from old stories, comparisons with others, or "shoulds?" For example, "I should be further along in my career by now," or "I should be more outgoing." Many of the shoulds come from cultural or family expectations. Take a moment and ask yourself if this is really what you want. You do have the power to reclaim and pivot your life and leadership, and you have the option to align what you want with your authentic self. Consider letting go of your shoulds.

- **Making the impossible possible.** This is the process of achieving what seems to be an unattainable goal—requiring you to uncover your buried dreams, identify the main obstacles in your way, and create a plan to achieve what you want.

How do you do this?

- Identify your top obstacle and take responsibility for navigating around it. This will require you to dig deep and uncover and manage any negative thoughts, emotions, or influences that could keep you from achieving your goal.

- Seek advice and support from like-minded people. Recruit a support team to help you reach your goal.

- Consider creative solutions, break your goals into smaller chunks, be open to changing your plan if needed, track your progress, continually visualize your goals to stay motivated, and see any obstacles as a test of your strengths instead of permanent roadblocks.

Power gap #3

Power gap: Failing to back yourself or ask for what you require or deserve.

Mindsets to close this power gap:

- **Harnessing the power of internal reference**. This refers to your ability to go with your gut feeling to make decisions. How much importance do you place on having your own opinion and deciding things on your own?

  How do you do this?

  - Take the Fingerprint for Success assessment and learn your preferences for internal reference.

  - Explore, strengthen, and stand for what you know and believe. Develop your awareness of what you know and your personal truths, and practice using them in your decision making.

  - Trust your gut more often and notice how helpful this is in becoming more decisive, influencing others, and living an authentic and meaningful life.

- **Having courage**. In the context of this book, courage is taking a risk or feeling afraid yet choosing to act anyway to follow a dream.

How do you do this?

- Become more comfortable making mistakes, which can start by celebrating your mistakes as opportunities to learn and noting the lessons they teach you.

- Focus on what you want, not your fears.

- Practice leaving your comfort zone, running toward your fears, and conquering them! Build up your courage muscles. Are you afraid of networking, posting to social media when your team wins an award, or speaking in public? Actively lean into situations or tasks that require courage. Start with small risks and let your momentum grow. See each new risk as an opportunity to grow and an adventure. Eventually, you will see yourself taking more and bigger risks to reach your dreams.

- **Asking for what you require or deserve**. This increases your self-esteem and is a sign that you are actively taking charge of your life. Taking a stand for yourself includes asking for what you need, which could include looking for a new job, negotiating for more resources or a salary bump, or recruiting a career sponsor who can speak for you at promotion time.

How do you do this?

- Know what you want or need at each step toward your goal. Get clear on your vision, your next steps, who can help you take each step. Be sure to tap into your network or support team.

- Have your "ask" in mind. This could be a question for someone, so that you have the information you need to complete your task, or it could be a request for an introduction to someone who could support your project in some way. Leaders can't accomplish goals without the help of others. Don't be afraid to ask for the help you need. Asking for resources or assistance does not make you weak. You might be surprised how many mentors, allies, career sponsors, supervisors, or people in your network want to help you accomplish your goals.

- Women often find it easier to take a stand, influence others, and make major decisions when it benefits others. Practice advocating for the needs of others if you want to build your negotiating skills.

Power gap #4

Power gap: Being uncomfortable making decisions, solving problems, setting goals, and using or developing your resources.

Mindsets to close this power gap:

- **Knowing and managing your personal power.** This refers to your ability to exert your influence, authority, and control to achieve a goal, complete a task, or communicate what is needed in a situation.

  How do you do this?

  - Take the Fingerprint for Success assessment and learn your preferences related to personal power. When you are comfortable with your personal power, you are confident in roles of influence, leadership, and navigating organizational politics.

  - Practice using your expertise and knowledge to make decisions and influence the decisions of others. Apply these two attributes to solve problems, set goals and priorities, gather resources, and make choices.

  - Break through any self-sabotaging "rules" and judgments about your personal power. Develop your presence by owning your "seat at the table." Understand how to influence people and discover healthy ways to compete. Master relationship building and learn how to manage the many stakeholders in your life, career, and business to get things done. Develop your commercial mindset early, and also develop your financial acumen. This might include managing budgets, and knowing the metrics used to measure success in your context.

- **Boosting your creativity.** This is your ability to come up with and recognize ideas to solve problems, communicate with others, or to challenge yourself or others.

How do you do this?

- Explore multiple solutions. Try looking at a variety of solutions and don't just rely on your standard approaches. Find inspiration to spark or start your solution building. This could include reading, visiting a library, and benchmarking how others have solved similar problems. Use the "snowball" technique, which starts with one idea, letting it lead to another idea, and connecting it with yet another idea. Creative solutions can come from combining great ideas.

- In solving problems or making decisions, brainstorm potential solutions. Start by suspending your judgment and self-criticism. Generate as many ideas as possible in a short time. Then clarify and refine your ideas until you find the one that works for you.

- As you gain confidence with your own creativity, challenge yourself by choosing new projects, using new tools, or collaborating with new partners.

- **Letting your imagination become the cornerstone of innovation.** Imaginative thinking is the process of forming new ideas, images, concepts, or objects. This leads to innovation, which is something new or changed that brings value. It can also be a new way of thinking or doing something. Innovation means different things in different contexts. If you seek variety or change of any kind, you will need to imagine it and probably find new ways to do things. When you consider a change, you typically consider how you can make a change so that it adds value to your life and the lives of others.

How do you do this?

- You can build your imagination by daydreaming, role playing, or visualizing. You can prime your imagination by observing people, playing, or finding something to stimulate your mind, thoughts, and senses.

- When imagining what it would be like to assume a new role or make a career shift, you can identify role models, conduct informational interviews, and consult mentors to learn more about what it is like to be in that role and what is required to be successful. Each of these strategies, and many others, help you explore the breadth of what might be required, model the behavior of effective leaders in the role, and experience with your senses how motivated you are to make that pivot.

- To learn or practice innovation, you can find ways to take risks and test your ideas through modest experiments. Spot opportunities to solve problems. Get in the habit of asking yourself, "How significant is this problem?" "Who benefits from solving this problem?" "Is it worth solving?" You never have enough time or resources to solve every problem, so prioritize. Use the minimum resources required to solve each problem by starting with a minimal solution and then build upon this.

Power gap #5

Power gap: Disconnecting from your strengths or isolating yourself from influential support.

Mindsets to close this power gap:

- **Leading change.** Leading change, with yourself or with others, requires you to create a bold vision and clear goals. Ensure your goals and the solutions you are designing are sustainable and fit into your lifestyle or within the culture of your family, workplace, or system. Secure support for the process, gather feedback or evidence of movement toward the goal, communicate regularly with relevant parties, and celebrate success along the way.

How do you do this?

- Leverage your strengths by connecting with the emotions that surface during any change process. Be authentic. Be open and trust your emotions at each step of the change process. Early on, you should focus on your dreams and what inspires you. Later in the process, you may experience vulnerability as you leave your comfort zone to innovate or embed new behaviors. You or others involved in the change may experience grief from the sense of loss that comes with change. It is important to be self-compassionate and empathetic to what is required to create change and to identify the "pain points" that must be healed or removed as part of the process. Don't hide your emotions. People don't trust what they don't understand, and this creates resistance. Authentic leaders bring people with them as they open and share all aspects of the change process.

- As you lead change, connect with those who can support the change. Be visible and inclusive in this process. Involve people at each stage and in all parts of your life, or the organization or system involved in the change. Gather feedback, insights, and ideas. There will be times when the energy of others will swell and boost yours—keeping the momentum or reducing the resistance.

- Do you resist change when you worry that taking on a new role, skill, or process will take you out of your comfort zone or make you vulnerable? Create the conditions for success by giving yourself and others additional time and training if necessary. Make space for learning, practicing, and adjusting. Be intentional about reflection. Set up systems to measure and evaluate the change. Remember to assess not just the outcomes of the change but also the impact of the change so you can understand the real value of the change.

- **Knowing your impact.** Look for ways to contribute to others in a way that is valuable to them.

How do you do this?

- Start by understanding what is important to others—your stakeholders. Collect feedback or information that highlights your contributions, achievements, and results.

- Learn to tell your story of contributions. Your story could describe who was involved, the challenges you faced, what you did to create the change, the results you achieved, and the difference the change made to others. Do this for yourself daily or weekly. Keep a spreadsheet or a journal. Document the ways you are changing and the ways you are leading change, and the difference that makes. This is a critical step in helping you internalize your change and support your change process.

- **Celebrating change.** Embrace the positive feelings that come from imagining a better future and the highs that come with the achievement of goals. These good feelings wire new habits into your brain. Celebrate with those people who supported the journey and created the change with you.

How do you do this?

- Regular celebrations of your wins brings you dopamine hits that make you feel happier. Monitor your results and celebrate often!

- Make it physical—use all your senses. For example, when you reach your goal, raise your voice and yell "YES!" in your mind, as it will raise your energy and spirits. Use a thumbs-up gesture to signal to those around you that someone did a great job. Let your feet dance under your desk. Or better yet, jump with joy! Celebrate in the moment, in private, or publicly. You choose.

- Make your celebration rewarding. Get a massage. Book a getaway adventure. Make your journey pleasurable and keep up the momentum by rewarding yourself along the way.

Five power pivots you can make

To close your power gap, you must make a **power pivot** and implement one or more strategies to close the gap to achieve your goals. Each power gap has a related power pivot and a success strategy. These power pivots represent shifts that are necessary for personal and leadership development. The five power pivots are:

1 **Awaken** to your power to lead and to inspire yourself and others.

2 **Activate** and initiate action and communication from strength, not fear.

3 **Advocate** for yourself and ask for and receive what you deserve.

4 **Amplify** your personal power, voice, and presence to influence yourself and others.

5 **Advance** yourself and others by appreciating your evolution, value proposition, and impact in the world.

To close your personal power gaps, identify the power gap you are experiencing and the related mindset that you must embody, and use the success strategy that will enable the power pivot you must make to accelerate toward your goals.

CLOSING YOUR POWER GAPS

POWER GAP	MINDSET TO CLOSE YOUR GAP	SUCCESS STRATEGY	POWER PIVOT
Not recognizing your strengths, and a sense of your value and impact	Clarity	Become clear on your strengths, power gaps, and power pivots.	Awaken to your power to lead and to inspire yourself and others.
Letting your fear hold you back from acting or communicating with strength	Confidence	Become confident and increase your self-esteem as you step into any opportunity or challenge.	Activate and initiate action and communication from strength, not fear.
Failing to back yourself or to ask for what you require or deserve	Courage	Use your call to courage and your inner wisdom to say "yes" and "no" to create the change required.	Advocate for yourself, and ask for and receive what you deserve.
Being uncomfortable making decisions, solving problems, setting goals, and using or developing your resources	Creativity	Take risks, experiment, consciously create, collaborate, and curate the choices that add value.	Amplify your personal power, voice, and presence to influence yourself and others.
Disconnecting from your strengths and isolating from influential support	Embrace, lead, and celebrate change	Reflect, reframe, re-vision, and leverage your results.	Advance yourself and others by appreciating your evolution, value proposition, and impact in the world.

Coming up, each chapter will focus on one of the five damaging power gaps that women experience, the mindsets you can develop and the strategies you can use to close each power gap, and the power pivots you can make on your pathway to powering up your leadership.

CHAPTER 5

AWAKEN

"Awakening is not changing who you
are but discarding who you are not."
DEEPAK CHOPRA

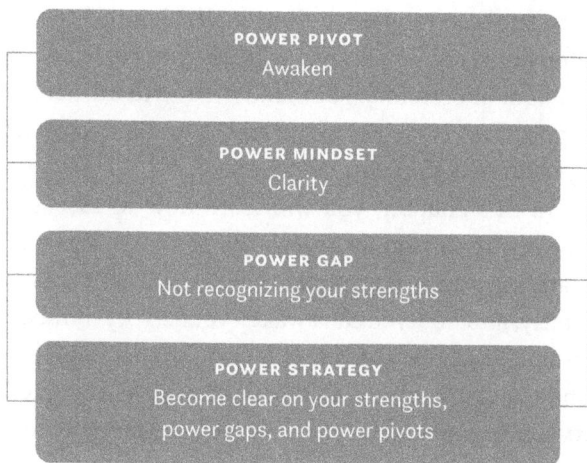

POWER PIVOT
Awaken

POWER MINDSET
Clarity

POWER GAP
Not recognizing your strengths

POWER STRATEGY
Become clear on your strengths,
power gaps, and power pivots

HAVE HAD many awakenings in my life, career, and in businesses I have led. During these moments, I found the clarity that comes when the clouds shift and the fog lifts after a storm. These awakenings come after I find myself off course—drifting. After talking with other female leaders who have navigated through their own personal storms, and through my experience and research, I have learned that daily practices and rituals enable me to maintain clarity and inspiration through rough seas.

For example, I have learned to develop my own internal compass, with the coordinates guided by my values, beliefs, sense of purpose, and personal truths to navigate me out of the fog. My compass is a personal manifesto that I have written, and I keep close for just these moments. As a result, I learned to quieten down my inner critic, who tends to come out in times of uncertainty. I befriend her and thank her for input. Then I take the wheel and steer the ship, so to speak, in the direction I need to go.

In this chapter, you will learn how to assess a power gap related to your clarity of vision. You will learn why clarity is important, what it feels like to lose clarity, and how you can awaken your clarity mindset to make a powerful pivot. By reframing your thoughts and tweaking this mindset, you can apply strategies to regain your clarity and close this power gap. You will learn the keys to clarity and powerful questions you can answer to accelerate yourself forward.

What does a clarity power gap feel like?

Some of us fall asleep to our vision, strengths, or connection to our power. Do you? It happens to us all. For
one reason or another, you fail to remember or recognize your strengths, which include your experience,
abilities, accomplishments, attitudes, ambitions, assertiveness, agency, and personal authority. This selec-
tive amnesia often includes what makes you special
or different, or your value. These are moments when
you lose sight of, don't experience, or disconnect
from your internal resources like inspiration, focus,
and determination.

In these moments, you may not even be aware that
you have a strength that matches what is needed in
the situation. You may not be aware of the depth and
breadth of your strengths. You may tell yourself that
you aren't good enough, smart enough, or creative
enough to get what you want or need. These stories
aren't true, and they limit your connections to your
strengths and talents. Whether you know it or not,
in these moments that you have disconnected from
your strengths, you are experiencing a power gap in
your clarity and you are letting your power leak away.

WHAT DO WOMEN EXPERIENCING THIS POWER GAP OFTEN SAY?

"I am not a leader."

"Who do I think I am to want this? I don't feel good enough."

"I am not ready to take on this role."

"I am unhappy, confused, feeling stuck, and unclear on what I should do next."

"I don't know what makes me special and valuable."

"I have no idea what I want in the future—I don't have ambition."

"I am burnt out and can't feel anything."

What are some examples of how you leak your power? There are so many ways that you can limit yourself and your vision of what is possible. Take time to deeply explore when you abandon yourself, give away your power, or let your power leave you temporarily. Which of these limiting beliefs are causing you to leak your power?

- Not recognizing your strengths and value.

- Not realizing the importance of having dreams and a life vision.

- Being overly focused on pleasing your boss or others and not yourself.

- Having difficulty sharing your opinions.

- Feeling getting the job done trumps taking care of yourself.

- Not being able to recognize your own needs.

- Wearing burnout, overwork, and overcommitment as a badge of honor.

- Struggling to set boundaries out of concern you will upset others.

- Worrying excessively what others think about you.

- Setting impossibly high standards for yourself and feeling you must be perfect.

- Feeling that you are not qualified for, or deserving of, your position or success, despite evidence to the contrary.

These are just a few examples of power gaps that you may experience, but there are many others. These power gaps are forms of self-sabotage and traps that snare, steal, or leak your power. While your lack of connection to your personal power can contribute to a lack of clarity, so too can external influences limit your vision of what is possible. Begin to awaken to the many factors that fog your vision and clarity. It's important for you to recognize when you are in a power gap that is within your immediate control to close and take steps to regain your power and clarity. Take the first step by adopting the awakened mindset.

The awaken mindset: clarity and inspiration

Successful female leaders are inspired by what they are creating and their vision for the future. They are awake to their vision for themselves and others and are raising their personal power through clarity and inspiration. In the awakening process, these leaders are using big-picture thinking, prioritizing, and eliminating distractions, aligning their inspiration and strengths with their vision for the future. They fuel their power to pivot toward their goals by consciously embodying their vision using all their senses—choosing what they think, see, hear, feel, and do as they move toward their goals. In this heightened state of self-awareness, they become pathfinders or pioneers, charting their course, using their internal compass as their guide.

Leaders with this capability are quick to spot the relevant issues that could get in their way and are adept at navigating around the obstacles. They are not weighed down by the details. In fact, the details are hard for them to see or can be demotivating. Big-picture thinkers are strategic. When you are creating a vision for what's next, it is important to avoid getting bogged down by any potential barriers and, instead, see the opportunities. Yes, it is important to understand the consequences of decisions and to consider risks, but these leaders do not let their negative mindsets, influences, or emotions drive them or hold them back.

When you are a big-picture thinker, you take time to feel into the frame, let yourself resonate with the potential paths ahead, and explore the options—making choices that resonate with your highest motivations, passions, values, and purpose.

Big-picture thinkers are motivated and inspired by their vision and ambition. If you are not excited or even a little scared about your vision for your future, or if you don't feel ambitious, your ideas may not be bold enough or you may have fears that are holding you back. When you are thinking strategically, and boldly, you are focused on the present moment and the future, and you are not stuck in the past. You navigate forward with a sense that the past brought you perspectives but does not define your future destination. Your failures teach you and prepare you—stretch you and strengthen you—yet you also feel boundless. You own your narrative, your context, and your choices.

Making the power pivot

When you fall asleep to your strength, you must awaken to your power to lead and inspire yourself and others. Each of us is in a constant state of awakening to ourselves. Awakenings are powerful points in time when your vision and clarity of direction combine with your passion, purpose, and inspiration. Awakenings occur when you embody your strengths and you are clear on what you want as well as what may be limiting you, such as outside influences, emotions, beliefs, or patterns of powerlessness. Awakenings can occur when you embody your strengths and actively clear those things that limit or cloud your vision. A point of awakening can also happen naturally, and you can then use it to intentionally raise your personal power, focus it, and accelerate yourself. These awakenings will drive you forward, and you benefit from learning to own, inspire, and manage your awakenings.

Awakening yourself is a process of raising your personal power by changing your state of mind or mindset and taking action to keep moving toward the goal. If you want to stay conscious of your personal power and avoid letting your power levels leak away, increase your clarity by focusing on your intent and purpose, inspiration, and big-picture thinking. Here are some practical ideas.

DAILY PRACTICES TO BOOST YOUR CLARITY

YOUR BODY

Fitness fix: Take regular work breaks, adding stretches, movement, music, or singing to your daily routine to raise your energy.

Mindful eating: If you typically skip breakfast, start your day with a meal to build your energy, and replace mindless snacking with healthier options.

Sleep schedule: Commit to a regular bedtime and wake-up time to give yourself enough sleep.

YOUR MIND

Find your power hours: Identify your most productive times of the day. Work on priority tasks during those times. You should also use this time to think about the big picture or projects requiring creativity or analytical thinking, not just small, random tasks.

Arrange to be inspired: Schedule "play" dates or time for those things in your life that inspire you.

Cultivate mindful moments: Carve out time to spend in silence, in nature, or doing activities that help you reflect and gain clarity. Use this time to set your intentions. Early mornings and just before bedtime are great times to form your intentions.

YOUR SOUL

Gratitude moments: Develop a routine around identifying and celebrating things you're grateful for. It can be quick, easy, and uplifting.

Body and soul check-in: Set a time to pause and acknowledge your emotions. Name your emotions. Act on what your emotions and your body are telling you.

Purpose prompt: Regularly write down your purpose for the day, week, or year. Put your prompt on a sticky note and paste it in a prominent location. Let your prompts keep you on point.

YOUR TIME

Celebrate your wins: Make time each day to note your wins. Embrace the high that comes with creating a win for yourself or others. Find ways to celebrate your milestones.

Power breaks: Schedule time to power up your mindset. On a scale of 1 to 5, rate your energy and clarity. When you feel depleted and need to boost your clarity, take a break, and take care of yourself in a way that powers you up!

Habit audit: At the end of the day, review the habits, including your mindsets, behaviors, and patterns, that supported or sabotaged your efforts. Practice habits that support you. Pivot away from habits that sabotage you.

Think about the points in your life when you have awakened, been inspired, and formed your vision and intention to make a change. Whether or not you were conscious of it at the time, you were making a power pivot in your life, career, or business. This pivot process requires you to dig deep inside yourself, raise your inspiration and energy for change, and conduct a series of experiments that move you toward your goals. With each experiment, you gain a bit more clarity about what is working or what isn't.

Examples of awakenings might be points of self-discovery of your strengths, talents, or ambitions. Or perhaps there was a time when a health crisis prompted you to focus on health and wellness or make your health a bigger priority in your life. Your awakening might have been related to a significant relationship in your life or a significant relationship change—marriage, birth, divorce, or death. Awakenings represent times when you felt clear on what you wanted, and you seized the moment and went for your goal. Awakenings come when you realize that change is required in your life, career, and business—and you recognize that your leadership, inspiration, and clarity must be aroused to focus yourself into thoughtful action.

Awakening moments can be powerful catalysts—inspiring you to act, pursue your goals with greater focus and determination, and tap into your full potential. These points of awakening often follow a significant power gap in one or more areas of your life that saw a significant change, challenge, or setback.

Awakenings can come from a "failure" that leads to learning and growth. Learn to embrace your failures and your awakenings.

Power mindsets and reframes

Awakenings are opportunities to take stock and develop or broaden your vision on what is possible and what could or should be accomplished. While it is important to be able to zoom in and see the details, it is also imperative that you step back or take a bird's-eye view of circumstances to determine what actions should be taken. Having the ability to view the big picture enables you to connect different pieces of the puzzle and to potentially take different and bigger leaps. Your ability to see the big picture allows you to create a vision for yourself and for others. It helps you amplify your ambitions and seize different opportunities because you don't get bogged down in the finer points or details.

Reframing is a technique you can use to shift your mindset so that you can see a different perspective or point of view, identify a false belief, free yourself if you feel stuck or want to change your perspective, or raise your energy or personal power. It enables you to look at yourself, a situation, a person, or a relationship in a different way. For this power pivot, you want to reframe to bring clarity and inspiration. Reframing helps you remember that your initial thought, conclusion, or explanation may not be the only point of view. Reframing shifts your patterns of thinking and believing, which can be negative or biased. If you are experiencing inconsistent results, feeling stuck, or not experiencing the momentum you desire, use reframing to uncover and clear damaging or limiting thought patterns. Do you have any of the following damaging thought patterns? If so, you can learn to disrupt or reframe these patterns.

Reframe Your Thoughts and Beliefs

DAMAGING PATTERNS OF THINKING
Personalization

DESCRIPTION
Taking things personally

Assuming responsibility for factors beyond your control

REFRAME
Ask yourself, "Am I allowing other people's remarks, actions, emotions, or behaviors to offend or affect me?"

"What are the facts in this situation and what are my assumptions?" Learn to separate the facts from the assumptions and let go of your assumptions.

Be compassionate with yourself and others. Ask, "What can I learn from this?" Use this situation as a moment to develop your growth mindset and emotional agility.

DAMAGING PATTERNS OF THINKING
Inner critic

DESCRIPTION
Your inner critic is the voice inside your head with nagging thoughts and negative self-talk. The critic represents your limited thinking, which limits your actions and communication. This pattern of thoughts grows unconsciously within you.

REFRAME
Recognize the voice of your critic.

Know that the critic comes with your fears. Most of the critic's observations are not true or helpful. Acknowledge them and then instruct the critic to step back.

Get curious and ask yourself what is causing or triggering the fear. The critic thinks they are protecting you and comes with an unhelpful core belief that can be cleared or discredited by noting the objective evidence.

You can learn how to use powerful reframes to gain clarity, increase your confidence, or have the courage to decide on or take your next step. It is not arrogant or selfish to appreciate your strengths or to see the situation through a better lens. Imagine the power and momentum that can be created by adding clarity to your vision and ambition. What are you doing to align your dreams and motivations with your life, career, and business design? It is time to wake up, check in, and consciously design your life, career, and business to be congruent with your highest self and highest purpose. Imagine the power of awakening to your true desires.

Strategies for closing this power gap

Closing this power gap requires you to find clarity, which accelerates you forward. You raise your personal power when you have a strong connection to your internal resources—mental states, mindsets, beliefs, and ways of seeing yourself, others, and the world around you. The path to finding your personal power is to let go of the self-judgments and habits that limit you, and to embrace your authentic self. This path leads to you finding your self-worth, establishing loving boundaries, and developing resilience.

You can experiment with strategies that help you stay conscious of your personal power levels to avoid letting them leak away, and to sustain your vision and intention. It is a daily and moment-to-moment process to stay conscious of your personal power. HeatherAsh Amara describes this daily practice as "maintaining a sacred container of awareness" that holds you while you consciously clear out the beliefs, stories, fears, emotions, and patterns that "clog" your system and leak your power.

One way to support high levels of your personal power or to maintain your power zone is to write and revise your personal manifesto, which outlines your aspirations, intended actions, achievements, and impact in the world. This manifesto guides your passions, purpose, values, and life rules. A personal manifesto is a written statement of your "why" that can serve as a guide to decisions and choices you want to make in your life, career, or business. Simon Sinek popularized the importance of knowing your "why" in his viral TED Talk. Your "why" describes with clarity what fulfills you and brings you meaning. Your manifesto should include a statement of how you define and measure your success. The Japanese refer to knowing your purpose as your "ikigai," which translates to "reason for being." What is the purpose of knowing your "why?" It lights you up and inspires you when it links your personal motivations to helping others. Your purpose focuses you on your goals and progress and lifts your confidence. Your purpose allows you to find meaning from trauma, loss, and setbacks, and to build your resilience.

I keep my manifesto on my laptop, and I refer to it often. It evolves as I learn and grow. My manifesto reminds me of my intentions and maintains my clarity. When I read it, I reawaken to my inspiration. It helps me reframe my mindset when needed. Here's a small section of it.

MY MANIFESTO

I am guided by my mission, values, purpose, and personal truths.

My **mission** is to enable personal and organizational growth and transformation for leaders, creating a better future for all. Specifically, I help founders and leaders start up and scale up their commercial ideas, careers, and ventures, while fostering respect, equity, diversity, inclusion, and innovation.

My values are inspiration, making ideas and actions possible, intuition, imagination and innovation, inclusion, and impact.

My **purpose** is to help women, particularly those in leadership, know themselves, grow their aspirations, and reach their dreams.

My **personal truths** are to remain:

- **Clear** on my intentions, curious, imaginative, playful, and inspired, experiencing the world with child-like discovery.

- **Confident** in my actions and communication, and focused on my passions, cutting away distractions, aligning with my purpose, reframing my negative emotions and beliefs, and ultimately raising my personal power.

- **Courageous**—by backing myself, asking for what I want, and being willing to receive what I deserve. I trust myself to solve the problems of life, career, and business by listening to my inner wisdom.

- **Creative**—by expressing myself through my voice, art, writing, and presence.

- **Celebratory** of my transformation—focused on my vision and delivering value and impact.

Keys to clarity for your power pivot

There are some keys to closing this power gap and making the power pivot to awaken to your power to lead and inspire yourself and others.

Give yourself permission to dream and see the big picture

Giving yourself permission to dream your dream is an essential step in the first power pivot. When you allow yourself to dream big, you expand your vision for what is possible in your leadership, life, career, and business. It helps you tap into your creativity and imagination and allows you to envision a future that excites and inspires you.

Are you struggling with giving yourself permission to dream your dreams? If so, you may have limiting beliefs or negative self-talk that holds you back from fully exploring your potential. Do you fear failure or judgment from others, or feel guilty for prioritizing your dreams over your other responsibilities?

To overcome these barriers, it is important to recognize that dreaming is not a frivolous or self-ish act. It's an essential part of the creative process that can lead to real-world success and fulfillment. When you give yourself permission to dream, you are opening yourself up to new possibilities and opportunities that can transform your life. Don't be afraid to dream big and give yourself permission to explore your potential. Set aside time to reflect on what you truly want, visualize your ideal future, and take steps toward making it a reality. Remember, your dreams are valid and achievable if you are willing to act on them and believe in yourself.

Know your definition of success

Success will look different for different women at different times in their life, career, or business. Take time to develop your own definition of success and align your leadership goals with what success means for you. Release the measures of success that were handed down to you by your grandparents, parents, and teachers. Go inside your heart, be inspired, and develop your own measures for success.

Consciously defining your success brings clarity and is inspiring. Being able to visualize your success is also essential to defining and growing your ambition. Seeing the big picture, which you have defined, will accelerate you. The process of defining your version of success and how you will measure success is the pathway to authentic leadership.

Develop a compass for your leadership

Knowing your personal truths is essential to authentic leadership and forming your own leadership style. When you embody your authentic leadership style, you are more satisfied, productive, and effective. Anchoring your personal truth in your body and your mind is as essential as having a compass, GPS system, or chart to map your current location and your destination. Developing clarity on your personal truths or compass for decision making is a powerful way for you to align your actions with your values and priorities. This involves creating a personal manifesto, as discussed earlier, or a set of guiding principles that define who you are and what you stand for. Here are some steps that you can take to develop your compass.

- **Reflect on your beliefs.** Consider your beliefs about yourself, others, and the world. Are these beliefs limiting or empowering? Do they align with your values and priorities? Are there any beliefs that you want to change or shift?

- **Write your personal manifesto.** This document is based on your values, beliefs, and principles that define who you are and what you stand for. Your manifesto should be concise, clear, and inspiring, and include your passion, purpose and intended impact on the world. Your personal manifesto should remind you of your unique value proposition. That is, what makes you different and valuable to yourself and to others.

- **Writing your values and your value proposition brings you clarity and is a place to return to when you want to reconnect with your strengths.** Seeing your capabilities more clearly will enable you to take a deeper look at your potential life, career, and business options or trajectories, providing you with more choices and your own compass to map your next steps. Your manifesto should also include your principles for operating and the mindsets that you want to demonstrate daily. It should also identify any emotions, beliefs, and behavioral patterns that you're aware of that limit your success and state your intention to adopt more successful patterns and to release any negative influences.

- **Have fun developing your manifesto and listing your unique superpowers and the value propositions you bring to the world.** This manifesto will help you understand your uniqueness, including any rough edges, shadows, and imperfections. Use this manifesto when you are feeling confused about a decision you want to make, preparing for a job interview, or having a new insight about your personal power. Your manifesto is a tool to power up—use it when you need to move out of your comfort zone to create a new future for yourself and others.

- **Use your compass to guide your decisions**. Your internal compass will point you toward the right choices in your leadership, life, career, and business. When you are faced with an opportunity, ask yourself, "Does this opportunity align with my values and priorities? Will this decision bring me closer to my goals and aspirations? Is this opportunity in line with my personal manifesto?" Listening to your internal compass will also help you stay focused and motivated as you work toward your goals and aspirations.

Tap into your resources to power up your leadership

You have internal and external resources you can use to achieve your goals. Tapping into your personal internal resources is an essential step in the first power pivot, as it helps you find inspiration and motivation from within. Here are some ways you can do that:

- **Focus on your strengths.** Appreciate your strengths and focus on them and not your deficits. When you focus on what you do well, you are more likely to feel capable and confident. Embody these elements—they are your superpowers.

- **Cultivate self-awareness**. Take time to reflect on your strengths, mindsets, and personal patterns. Develop daily rituals that help build your self-awareness. Use the ideas detailed in the "Daily Practices to Boost Your Clarity" table, mentioned earlier in this chapter, to boost your self-awareness.

- **Learn to know your emotional states**. Develop a repertoire of strategies to change your states to enable you to achieve your intended goals and outcomes. Identify the personal patterns that are limiting you and change them.

- **Visualize your success.** Take time to visualize yourself succeeding in your goals and aspirations. Visualization builds your clarity, which leads to confidence and courage. Write down your vision. Post it where it can inspire you. Use an online tool like Pinterest or Canva, or pull out some magazines, markers, and a glue stick to create a vision board. Fill it with images and words that spark the emotions that accelerate you forward. Fuel up your vision with your emotions.

- **Embrace your emotions, fears, and failures**. Recognize these as a natural part of learning and leading. Leadership models from the past taught us to take emotions out of the equation. Your emotions help you understand situations if you listen to them. Get to know your emotional landscape. With practice, or with the help of a coach, you can recognize when your emotions are blocking you from achieving your goals. When you let fear grow and become a block to your forward momentum, it is harder to learn, lead, and achieve. When you view failure as an opportunity to learn and grow, you bounce back more quickly and are more confident. Learn from your fears. Reframe failure and make it part of your growth strategy.

- **Practice vulnerability.** Embrace vulnerability by sharing your thoughts, feelings, and ideas with others. Ask for help or for what you need. When you allow yourself to be vulnerable, you open yourself up to new experiences and connections, which are sources of inspiration and courage for yourself and others. Sharing yourself with others builds trust and authenticity. Brené Brown, in her book *Daring Greatly*, defines vulnerability as leading and acting, despite uncertainty, risk, and emotional exposure. Be willing to show up as your authentic self even though you know you cannot control the outcomes of your actions.

- **Take small steps.** Taking one step after another outside your comfort zone builds your vision, inspiration, confidence, and momentum for bigger goals and aspirations.

- **Practice self-care.** Engage in activities that nourish your mind, body, and soul connection. This can include things like exercise, meditation, reading, art, music, dance, or spending time in nature. When you take care of yourself, you feel more personal power, energy, focus, and inspiration to take on new challenges. Self-care includes cultivating self-compassion. Be kind and compassionate toward yourself. When you treat yourself with kindness and understanding, it can help you feel more inspired and resilient. Develop a self-care routine that nourishes you with inspiration, connection, and fun.

- **Seek out positive role models and relationships.** Surround yourself with people who uplift and support you. Connect with friends, family, or colleagues who share your values and goals. Their encouragement and feedback can be a source of fuel and inspiration. Know your goals and ambitions, and recruit a support team to cheer you on. Choose mentors, career sponsors, and coaches who will provide the support you need to achieve the success you desire.

POWERFUL QUESTIONS THAT ACCELERATE YOU!

Before we move on, here are some questions I'd like you to think about:

1   What is your definition of success?

2   What does your definition of success imply for your new goals or a pivot in your leadership, life, career, or business development?

3   What are the personal truths that will guide your leadership, life, career, or business decisions?

4   What are the internal resources that you will leverage regularly in your leadership, life, career, and business?

5   What support do you need to help you achieve the goals you have set? Who will you recruit for your support team?

Power affirmation: I inspire myself.

CHAPTER 6

ACTIVATE

"For me, the process of embodying confidence
was less about convincing myself of my own
worth and more about rejecting and unlearning
what society has hammered into me."

LINDY WEST

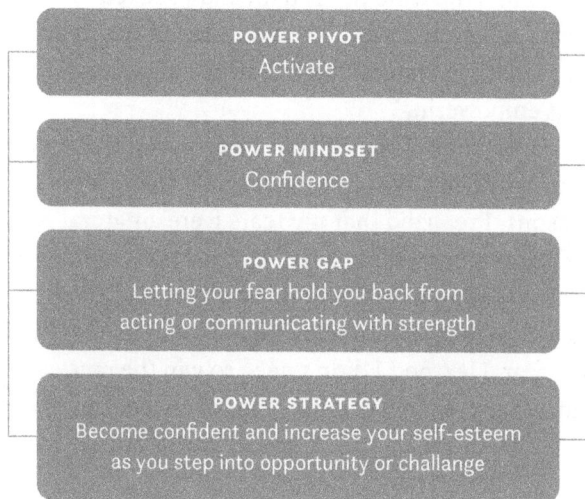

POWER PIVOT
Activate

POWER MINDSET
Confidence

POWER GAP
Letting your fear hold you back from
acting or communicating with strength

POWER STRATEGY
Become confident and increase your self-esteem
as you step into opportunity or challange

IT IS NATURAL to be afraid when you are leading, making decisions, or solving problems with very little information in a constantly changing world. However, you can't let your fear hold you back or keep you frozen in place. Does your fear have a hold on you? Do you believe that you lack confidence—and that it's standing in the way of your success?

I learned that I couldn't wait to be confident before I went after my dreams. When I decided to learn to sail, I was terrified. I remember walking to the yacht club; my heart was racing. I was so nervous I almost turned around and went home. But I knew I needed to face my fears if I wanted to learn how to sail. When I arrived at the dock, my instructor did his best to put me at ease. He showed me the ropes and the basics of sailing. As we set sail for the first time, I could feel the wind in my hair, and I started to relax. I was still scared but I was also excited. I was learning something new and going after a dream, and that was empowering.

At the end of the lesson, I was proud that I had faced my fears. Was I confident, yet? No! After many lessons, I realized that my fears were a natural part of learning something new. I learned that confidence was a feeling or state of mind that I had to claim, like a prize given for showing up and pushing past my fear. I learned I didn't need to win the race each time; I just needed to climb aboard my boat and join the race. The key is just starting—activating yourself, taking the initiative, and pivoting in a new direction.

In this chapter, you will learn what a confidence power gap feels like, and how to activate the mindsets of confidence and initiation to make a power pivot. I will show you the keys to confidence for your power pivot that I have learned from my own experience and the experiences of other women. Finally, you will be prompted to answer powerful questions in relation to this power pivot.

What does a confidence power gap feel like?

You know you are experiencing this power gap if you can feel inside your body that you are holding back. You can recognize that you have a need to speak or act, but somehow you feel frozen. This feeling comes from your fear. You hear the critical conversations happening around you, but you are not joining the conversation. You see the opportunity, but you feel frightened; you feel like hiding or running or you feel yourself closing down. You see yourself withdrawing or standing back. You hear yourself not speaking your truth. This gap also shows up when you go on autopilot and let opportunities pass you by, over and over. You are in this power gap when you experience yourself in a state of denial, procrastination, or resignation.

WHAT DO WOMEN EXPERIENCING THIS POWER GAP OFTEN SAY?

"I need to gather more information before I make a decision."

"Everyone in my family is an engineer. There was no choice; I became an engineer. Now, I am just going to keep pushing through, but this job is soul crushing."

"I can't take on that role; I don't have quite enough experience."

"I don't feel comfortable sharing my ideas because they aren't popular with management."

"I don't have what she has, so why bother?"

"I am not going to ask for help. I should be able to do this."

"If I ask for help, they will think I am weak or stupid."

"I have tried that before, and it never works."

"I have been dreaming about starting my own business for years, but I just don't think I can make it happen—it would mean making too many changes in my life."

What are some examples of how you leak your power? You hold yourself back, keep yourself small, or avoid action because of your negative beliefs or emotions. You may not consciously realize that you are not acting from a place of personal power. Here are a few examples of when you are experiencing a power gap or leaking personal power:

- You prefer not to work outside your comfort zone, or when the situation brings uncertainty or requires you to leverage new or different capabilities.

- Continually, you feel wrong, not ready, ashamed, guilty, or that you are a failure.

- You are fearful of being exposed as a fraud and you lack confidence in your abilities, despite your education, years of experience, and solid performance in the past.

- Often you doubt and second-guess yourself.

- Regularly, you feel like you are not good enough to achieve your goals.

- You have a sense of powerlessness, which leads to procrastination, inaction, or not speaking your truth or asking for what you need.

- You compare yourself to others and feel like you are not measuring up, or feel jealous or insecure.

- You prefer to follow orders or execute requests without question, or you are deferential in decision making even when you have your own preferences, needs, or ideas to contribute.

- You look for validation from others or you let others dictate the direction of your life, career, or business.

- You see yourself seeking to please others regardless of the cost.

- Regularly, you have trouble speaking your truth in the face of authority or sharing an unpopular opinion.

- You avoid taking a visible leadership role.

- Often you feel like you don't belong, driving you to never stand out, take risks, or make mistakes.

- You do not trust your own experience.

- You are unable to manage your time or your habits to achieve your goals.

The activate mindset: confidence and initiation

Women demonstrate a mindset of confidence when they initiate action and communicate from strength and not fear, and adopt the mindset of *impossible to possible*. This mindset is crucial to success in uncertain circumstances. From the outside, these women display a can-do attitude. They are not afraid to take risks and are comfortable with uncertainty. They are also able to bounce back from setbacks and failures. Leaders who are focused on their goals, and who initiate and make the impossible possible, are compelling and attract success. There is very little time between the moment they set a goal and the time they take action to make their inspiration a reality. Leaders who are highly motivated to initiate act quickly and rarely procrastinate. Leaders with this mindset experiment with strategies while moving quickly toward their goals with a sense of confidence. They know they can think on their feet. When you have this mindset, you move ahead without necessarily having a great deal of prior experience and work out your challenges and next steps as you go.

When you are fully activated, filled with clarity and confidence, you know that you don't need to have all the details worked out ahead of time or have a fully fleshed out plan. You proceed knowing that you will make the power pivots required in the moment as you move toward your goal. Leaders in this zone of power prefer to act or to speak up and they aren't afraid of failure. In fact, they see failure as part of the learning process and use "fast failure" as their way forward toward success. They don't want to miss opportunities in life, career, or business. The power strategy these women use is to become confident through action and opportunities that challenge them. How motivated are you to seize opportunities, or put your ideas into action?

Making the power pivot

The success strategy for this power pivot is to become more confident and increase your self-esteem as you step into any opportunity or challenge. When you are in your power zone making powerful pivots, you are operating at your highest level of personal power and can achieve your goals in life, career, and business.

Here are some examples of what being in your power zone looks like (for women in particular):

- You are pursuing your passion, whether it's through your career, a creative pursuit, or a personal project. You are in alignment with your values and personal truth, and can stay focused, motivated, and productive.

- You have been working in the same job for years and decide to apply for a promotion, even though you are not sure you are ready for it. You recognize that there will be uncertainty and challenges in taking on a new role, but you also know that you have the skills and determination to succeed.

- You are balancing multiple roles, such as motherhood and a career. You don't always get it right, but, overall, you can prioritize your time and energy effectively, staying present and engaged in most areas of your life.

- You are changing careers midlife, whether to pursue a passion or to seek a more fulfilling job. This can involve going back to school, starting at the bottom of a new field, and facing uncertainty about the future. However, by leveraging your skills and strengths, you know that you can make a successful transition and find a new career that brings you joy and satisfaction.

- You make a power pivot by leaving a toxic or abusive relationship. This can involve facing fear and uncertainty about the future, rebuilding your life and identity, and finding the strength to make a change. By recognizing your own worth and taking action to protect yourself, you can make a successful pivot and find a happier, healthier life.

- You are a successful entrepreneur, running your own team, department, or business, and you are making a difference in your industry and community. You are confident in your abilities, and you use your strengths to drive your success. You have dreamed of starting your own business and you decide to take the leap despite not having a lot of experience or financial resources. You know that the road ahead will be challenging, but you have hope and optimism in equal measure, and are willing to experiment, take risks, and learn from your mistakes.

- You are leading in your organization, inspiring, and empowering your team to achieve their goals. You can communicate effectively, make decisions confidently, and handle challenges with relative ease.

When women are in their power zone and making a power pivot, they tap into their potential and achieve their goals with confidence. In all of these examples, you are embracing uncertainty and acting despite the possibility of failure. You believe in yourself and your abilities, and you are willing to put in the work to achieve your goals. This mindset can be incredibly powerful in helping you to succeed in all areas of your life.

Power mindsets and reframes

This power pivot will require you to give up a damaging habit, emotional state, or distorted thinking pattern to gain what you want. By reframing, you can discover and discern if the power pivot means making an internal change or an external change. You can assess whether your situation or context is affecting your self-esteem, or whether an internal state of mind is eroding your confidence and sense of possibility. If you discover that the gap making you feel powerless is coming from within you, you can, with practice and focus, reframe yourself into a more powerful position to experience success. Identify if you have any of these habits or negative mindsets and start working today to reframe them.

Reframe Your Thoughts and Beliefs

DAMAGING PATTERNS OF THINKING
Fixed mindset

DESCRIPTION
If you have this mindset, you believe that your intelligence, capabilities, and talents are fixed at birth. This mindset inhibits risk taking and problem solving, and provokes feelings of dissatisfaction, disappointment, and stagnation. It may decrease your self-knowledge and self-awareness.

REFRAME
Make it a habit to get out of your comfort zone. Take on new projects that require you to learn and experiment. Look for challenges that inspire you. Befriend your fear and move toward it instead of moving away from it.

Make friends with feedback, too. Redefine your definition of failure and recognize that it is required for learning, growth, and innovation.

Surround yourself with people who have different perspectives and who inspire you. Recognize that change and growth come in small steps. Let the inspiration pull you forward.

DAMAGING PATTERNS OF THINKING
Negative beliefs or stories about yourself

DESCRIPTION
Humans create meaning through stories. Something happens and you make up a story to explain the situation and the results. As your mind is processing, it taps into your past, including your thoughts, beliefs, emotions, and stories that have been stored in your unconscious mind. This is instinctual and is a way your mind tries to keep you safe. However, if these stories become negative, self-critical, or limiting, they can be cleared or reframed.

REFRAME
Reframe your negative or biased stories by catching them and challenging them.

Ask, "Is this story or belief true? Are there other plausible explanations?"

Rewrite or reframe your stories and quiet the negative voice or "inner critic." Clearing these negative beliefs, and developing or replacing them with positive beliefs, will be inspiring, increase your capability to initiate action and communication, and lift your confidence.

DAMAGING PATTERNS OF THINKING
Self-abandonment

DESCRIPTION
Self-abandonment occurs when you ignore your needs or emotions or hide parts of yourself to get your needs met or approval from others.

REFRAME

Start by becoming self-aware of when this happens and understand what this negative thought and behavior pattern costs you.

Begin making yourself a priority in your decision making. This takes practice and is a balancing act when you are responsible for others.

Practice self-compassion.

Allow yourself to be creative, quirky, and uniquely you.

Surround yourself with those whom you trust and who support you.

DAMAGING PATTERNS OF THINKING
Focusing on things that are outside of your control

DESCRIPTION
You can increase your sense of power and personal agency by focusing on what you can control and letting go of anything that is out of your direct control.

REFRAME
Learn to spot which aspects of a situation are within your control. Your reaction or behavior are within your control. There are situations that trigger and evoke emotional responses based on your insecurities. Learn to recognize your triggers and how to reframe your reactions to these triggers.

Sharon Melnick, PhD, in her book *Success Under Stress*, shares research about focusing on the fifty per cent that you can control. That is, your reaction to the work bully, your judgment about what others are thinking of you, your deflation because you don't feel heard, the boundaries you set when you share your truth, or the frustration you feel when others don't cooperate in important relationships.

DAMAGING PATTERNS OF THINKING
Disqualifying the positive

DESCRIPTION
Ignoring or invalidating all the good things that you have achieved or compliments that you have received.

Forgetting about your strengths, experience, and accomplishments.

Fearing your authority, agency, assertiveness, or ambition.

REFRAME
Disqualifying the positive undermines your confidence and sense of possibility.

Reframe by understanding when you are disqualifying your positive attributes, or positive comments or compliments that come your way.

Identify any negative beliefs or thought patterns that are associated with getting compliments. These thought patterns are likely linked to negative beliefs or feelings. You don't have to believe everything you feel. Look at the facts and embrace your positive traits and accomplishments.

Practice receiving and internalizing positive feedback.

Learn to be able to talk about your progress or impact.

Regularly take note of what you or your team accomplished during that day or that week.

Collect thank-you notes, positive feedback, and information that lets you know you are making progress. Keep it in a file or somewhere visible, like on the refrigerator.

When someone asks you how you are doing, reply with a sentence or two about your goal, what you are working on now, and your "progress report."

DAMAGING PATTERNS OF THINKING
All-or-nothing thinking

DESCRIPTION
You don't see the gray or the middle ground. You tend to see things in black or white. You don't believe in mistakes, preferring to believe that you must be perfect.

REFRAME
All-or-nothing thinking, sometimes called black-and-white thinking, kills your confidence.

Reframe your view and practice looking for the middle ground. Change your vocabulary to use "and" instead of "or" and "but." For example, "I made progress this week and I had a setback." Begin using the word "yet" more often, too. For example, "I have yet to learn that skill." Reframe your language and you can reframe your brain to feel more confident.

DAMAGING PATTERNS OF THINKING
Mind reading

DESCRIPTION
Mind reading is the act of assuming what someone else is thinking.

REFRAME
This negative thought pattern erodes your confidence.

Begin to observe how you perceive, interpret, and respond to the thoughts and emotions of others. Attune yourself to those instances when you are predicting what others are thinking and feeling. Reframe yourself and question your accuracy. Evaluate the cost and benefit of mind reading. You may think that your mind reading is protecting you from a bad outcome, but it costs you with increased anxiety, self-consciousness, rumination, and possibly depression.

Catch yourself when you mind read. Question your accuracy of predicting others' thoughts and interrogate the costs and benefits. While mind reading can be accurate in some situations, this thought pattern often harms you more than it protects you. Disrupt this pattern.

DAMAGING PATTERNS OF THINKING
Jumping to conclusions

DESCRIPTION
You believe that you are a mind reader and know what other people are feeling or thinking, and you make judgments or adopt behaviors accordingly.

REFRAME
With practice, you can reframe or break this habit by unpacking your assumptions, and identifying alternative explanations for what is happening.
You can reframe this negative mindset or habit by building your capability for reflection and patience. Take time between the stimulus and your response. Actively create time to reflect, reframe, and learn from this practice.

DAMAGING PATTERNS OF THINKING
Procrastination

DESCRIPTION
If you are a chronic procrastinator, you avoid tasks, may prefer distractions, and struggle with self-control. This non-action may also bring on negative emotions. Some procrastinators are perfectionists who avoid taking risks.

REFRAME
Reducing or eliminating procrastination will boost your confidence.

We procrastinate because we don't believe we will enjoy the task, or we may not believe we will complete the task well or successfully.

Recognize the costs of procrastination. What happens when you routinely put off tasks or fail to complete them?

Keep goals realistic, break projects into smaller tasks, make time for projects you are putting off, and set yourself firm deadlines.

DAMAGING PATTERNS OF THINKING
Emotional reasoning

DESCRIPTION
You believe that your emotions and what you are feeling are always and automatically true. When you practice emotional reasoning, you are interpreting your situation through your feelings.

For example, you feel anxious, so therefore you feel there is danger.

REFRAME
Give yourself permission to have the feeling.

Slow your thoughts and bring yourself back to more realistic perceptions.

Begin to pause in emotional situations to allow the emotion to pass through your body. Honor and fully embody your emotion. When the emotion has passed through you, recheck your body, your feelings, and your assumption.

Remember that you are not your emotions.

You can recognize your emotions and learn from them. Look below the emotion to learn more.

For example, if you feel worthless, not good enough, or shame, you can ask yourself what evidence supports or contradicts this feeling.

Strategies for closing this power gap

Closing this power gap requires you to find and grow your confidence and self-esteem as you step into any challenge or opportunity. These strategies require you to act and communicate from strength, not fear.

Powering up your confidence takes practice. You must be able to understand your context, needs, goals, and the appropriate actions in different situations. Understanding how to operate from strength, not fear, will help you develop self-awareness, including your ability to spot your thought, emotional, and behavioral patterns, triggers, and the contexts.

How do you spot negative thought, emotional, and behavioral patterns?

- Identify any automatically forming negative patterns. Form a list. Look at their frequency.

- Determine the consequences of the patterns.

- Break down the scenario that triggered the pattern into three parts—the details of the situation, your mood or thoughts, and the image/s that comes to mind.

- Actively change the negative pattern to a more productive one. In addition to the suggestions included in this book, you may consider working with a behavior therapist or coach to help you with this.

How do you identify your emotional triggers?

- A trigger is a telltale sign that leads to an unwanted and unexpected escalation of your emotions or thoughts. Identify examples of situations that lead quickly, automatically, and subconsciously to negative thought or emotional patterns. Understand that these triggers are unconscious reactions to experiences that are reminiscent of a painful feeling that, most likely, you first experienced in your childhood. When you were growing up, you may have suffered in some way in relation to an incident that you could not deal with sufficiently at the time. Now as an adult, you may encounter a situation that makes you recall that painful feeling you had as a child. You are triggered, even though the facts in the present situation do not perfectly match those from the past event.

- Examples of emotional triggers are feeling self-conscious when you enter a networking event, being discounted when someone interrupts you, feeling you are being controlled when someone makes a decision without telling you, feeling taken advantage of when you consistently are assigned the most unrewarding tasks, feeling vulnerable when you are asked to present something with little notice, and boundary concerns when someone uses aggressive language or behavior.

- These triggering situations can cause you to feel emotions like rejection and betrayal, the experience of unjust or unequal treatment, a sense of being excluded, ignored, unwanted or not needed, and a loss of independence or autonomy.

- Recognize these triggers by listening to your body and looking for signs of a pounding heart, upset stomach, dizziness, shakiness, and sweat.

- Take the situation and break it down into its parts. For example, what happened first, second, and third? Consider the content of the situation, the tone, and the environment. Reflect in detail. Be honest with yourself.

- Determine how you are going to act. Are you going to try to remove your trigger, or reframe your thoughts, emotions, or behaviors in reaction to the trigger? In some situations, you can work with yourself or with the help of a therapist to remove your triggers. In other situations, you may choose to talk with the people involved in the triggering behavior. Use what you have learned about how to communicate without fear to begin a conversation with those involved. Share the details of your experience so the others involved can understand the situation and the impact. Brainstorm how you can ensure the situation doesn't happen in the same way again, and discuss how you can support each other as you learn from trying new approaches that are less triggering.

How do you identify negative or toxic contexts?
Contexts differ greatly, but here are a few signs of toxic work environments:

- Poor communication, lack of transparency, and vague or undefined roles.

- No respect or opportunities for input.

- Normalizing and rewarding overwork, unhealthy competition, poor or no boundaries, celebrating "stars" and identifying scapegoats.

- Evidence of in-groups, cliques, exclusion, gossip, and bullying.

- Low morale, enthusiasm, or satisfaction among employees.

- High turnover, fatigue, and illness due to stress and burnout.

- Unfair policies, unequal enforcement, and conflicts or grievances not being handled properly.

- Arbitrary or non-existent performance reviews.

- Non-existent or ineffective diversity, equity, and inclusion initiatives.

- Narcissistic leaders who do not care about or empathize with co-workers or other staff.

It is worth repeating that powering up your confidence takes practice. Understanding how to operate from strength and not fear is an essential part of leading your life, career, and business. Developing self-awareness is the first step here.

Keys to confidence for your power pivot

This power pivot requires you to stop sabotaging yourself by letting your fear and limiting beliefs hold you back, and instead raise your personal power to act or communicate from strength. There are some keys to closing this power gap and pivoting to the activate mindset so that you can make the impossible possible.

Claim your confidence

Understand your emotional landscape, your triggers, and your fears. Pinpoint the moments that drain or undermine your confidence and put strategies in place to get you back on the confidence track. Work with a coach to clear your negative beliefs, fears, and triggers, and to anchor your confidence in your body. Recognize when your "inner critic" is running the show and take her gently off stage. Your brain is wired for negativity and bias, and it takes practice to break these default, negative thinking patterns and claim your confidence. Keep a journal, list, or file on the positive feedback that you have received. Capture, retain, and refer to a list of your skills and accomplishments on a regular basis. Create your own strategies to claim your confidence—a song you play to increase your energy and confidence, a pair of power shoes you wear for presentations, a power pose you use just before a negotiation. Curate your confidence routine. Focus on and use your strengths and drop the focus on what you perceive are your "weaknesses."

Reframe the fears, negative beliefs, and emotions that hijack your confidence. Learn to recognize and challenge the limiting beliefs. If you are telling yourself that you aren't qualified, remember all the things that you have accomplished in life. Be deliberate, gather the evidence, and prove the belief isn't true and that you will overcome this limited thinking. Acknowledge that this belief is not a fact. Reframe your inner dialogue. Instead of saying to yourself, "I am not good at this," remind yourself, "As I practice, my skills will improve." Instead of saying, "I am too afraid to tackle this opportunity," coach yourself by saying, "Fear is natural, I can do this!" At first this takes practice, and it requires that you get in touch with your limiting beliefs.

It helps to keep track of any fears, beliefs, and emotions that block you. Journaling or logging your thoughts can help. Claiming your confidence also means claiming your ambitions and dreams—let them fuel you, inspire you, and pull you forward. Moonshot goals can rocket you to new heights.

Build self-trust

Connect with yourself by developing a deeper understanding of your true desires and longings, and practice care and compassion for yourself. Know your truth and back yourself. If you don't trust yourself, you may be abandoning yourself, driving yourself too hard without acknowledging yourself or your heart's desires. You may be in a toxic environment or have an unsupportive supervisor, team member or partner. Make decisions that support you. Be patient with yourself and eliminate any internal dialogue that does not support you and your confidence.

Choose your contexts and set boundaries or change your circumstances if the culture, environment, or people are not supportive. Know that whatever comes your way, you will be able to rise to the challenge. Learn to rely on your mental, emotional, and physical abilities. Cultivate your growth mindset and begin to see yourself as a resourceful problem solver and lifelong learner. Reframe your relationship with failure and begin to see life, career, and business as a series of experiments. You choose what is working and not working in any situation and you adjust. Respect your opinions and stand up for yourself if you are wronged. Avoid people who disrespect you, shame you, or belittle your truth.

Act with radical confidence

Believe that problems are solvable through action and direct communication. Practice radical confidence. Identify what is keeping you from acting and communicating from a point of strength. Don't procrastinate. Know your risk appetite and the risk appetite of those with whom you are working. Learn how to read situations, and to adjust your action and communication based on your context and the people involved (and their communication styles). Learn to appreciate that the level and tempo of action and communication when you are creating change, innovating, or starting up an initiative or business are different from those when you are scaling a tested process, product, or business. Acting in this way requires you to live and lead consciously.

Conscious leadership is the practice of being more aware as a leader. Conscious leaders are skilled in self-awareness and self-management, especially regarding their positive and negative emotions, beliefs, and influences, and how they impact the people they lead. This type of leadership focuses on introspection and intentionality. Conscious leaders speak with integrity, hold themselves responsible for their thoughts, actions, and impact, and lead with authenticity. Identify any negative emotions, beliefs, and influences that derail you, and begin to challenge them and release them. Notice what triggers you to lose your positive mindset and personal power. When you notice your thoughts, energy, or beliefs are taking a negative turn, consciously change them. Give yourself permission to play, take time with other tasks, or rest. Take radical responsibility to make a power pivot that might be required.

POWERFUL QUESTIONS
THAT ACCELERATE YOU!

Before we move on, here are some questions I'd like you to think about:

1. What beliefs do you hold about yourself or your leadership that limit you? What belief could you adopt instead? What stories have you developed about yourself that you can reframe or rewrite to make a power pivot?

2. What are some examples of when you let fear hold you back from acting or communicating with strength? What were the consequences? What is a power pivot you can make now to change that result next time you are in the same situation?

3. Describe the emotions that limit your leadership. What power pivot could you make to release these emotions?

4. What radical acts of confidence will you begin to consciously practice?

Power affirmation: I act and communicate confidently.

CHAPTER 7

ADVOCATE

"Fear is the chasm between where you are right now and where you want to be. Courage is the bridge that will help you cross it."

REBECCA RAY

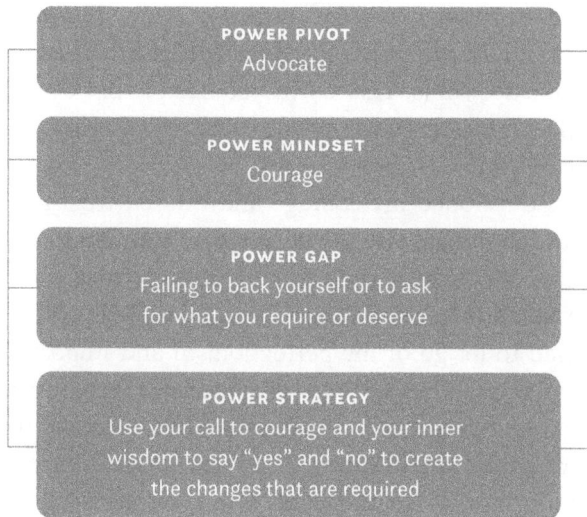

POWER PIVOT
Advocate

POWER MINDSET
Courage

POWER GAP
Failing to back yourself or to ask for what you require or deserve

POWER STRATEGY
Use your call to courage and your inner wisdom to say "yes" and "no" to create the changes that are required

DVOCATING FOR yourself means taking a stand and telling yourself and the world that you are worthy. It means that you ask for what you need or what you desire. It means that you make choices with yourself in mind—putting yourself first. This could mean listening to your deepest desires, hearing your inner voice that tells you when it is time to move on to a new relationship or job, or distancing from people in your life who want to criticize, disrespect, invalidate, blame you, or steal your time. When you advocate for yourself, you understand what you want, and what you will and will not accept.

You also advocate for yourself when you make a decision in the face of uncertainty, using the information you have in that moment. The world doesn't wait for you to gather more information, learn more, and thus make "perfect" decisions. You will rarely have all the information and knowledge you need to make decisions. This is why you need to back yourself—by trusting yourself and using your intuition to guide you.

I developed my courage and my self-trust as I learned to lean into my personal wisdom and intuition. What did I need to give up to advocate for myself and to ask for what I needed and deserved? I had to let go of my perfectionism and imposter syndrome. I needed to develop the capacity to leverage boundaries and my support team. I needed to strengthen my intuition and trust myself. Once I made this mindset shift, I felt a flood of courage flow through me. Deciding with my intuition, if that was all that was available at the time, made decisions easier and built a sense of momentum in my life.

In this chapter, you will learn what a courage power gap feels like. You will learn how to develop your advocate mindset, which connects you with your courage and intuition. You will learn how to uncover damaging patterns and develop power strategies to close this power gap. You will receive the keys to courage, which you can adopt in your life to make powerful pivots, and you will be asked a series of powerful questions.

What does a courage power gap feel like?

You may have grown up believing that courage is the absence of fear. Courage is acting, backing yourself or others, and asking for what you want or need *despite* the fear that you feel. Courage is your willingness to respond in the moment despite the negative thoughts or emotions running consciously or unconsciously inside of you. It is understanding that you may have worries, doubts, anxiety, or fear about taking a risk, but making choices and acting anyway. These emotions and thoughts come on stronger when you are exhausted or stressed. Listen to your body wisdom. Are you tensing up, feeling the temperature rise in your body, or hearing a ringing sound? Everyone's physical reaction to anxiety, stress, and fear is unique.

WHAT DO WOMEN EXPERIENCING THIS POWER GAP OFTEN SAY?

"I can't say 'no' to my boss."

"I know my team needs more resources, but I am afraid to ask for more."

"This role is not for me. It is too big a leap and I don't believe they will hire a woman."

"I have been doing great work and hitting all my targets. I am afraid to ask for a promotion. They just won't listen."

"Maybe, when things are calmer, I will look for a new role in a different organization."

"My job is soul crushing. I want to start up my own company. Every time I think about leaving my job, I push the decision into the future."

What are some examples of how you leak your power? There are times in your life, career, and business when you fail to back yourself. This behavior is a sign of a power gap. This power leak, like others, is often driven by a negative thought, belief, or influence. The gap may also be happening because of how you manage yourself, your thoughts, and your health, or how you prioritize yourself in decision making. Power gaps can happen unconsciously because you never had role models who advocated for themselves, or you haven't practiced asking for what you desire. You may not have taken the time to know what you need or what you desire.

Power gaps can also happen when you need to learn a new skill or adopt a new mindset. You can also experience a power gap if you believe that leaders cannot show humility or vulnerability or must be independent and resourceful—without engaging others in creating win-win solutions. You may be in an organization or system in which outdated leadership styles or toxic cultures pull you out of your power zone. Regardless of the sources of the power gap, you must identify the sources and close the gap. This step will require you to advocate for yourself, perhaps for the first time. Here are some examples of when you are failing to advocate for yourself. You are experiencing a gap when you:

- Decide not to negotiate for a higher salary or promotion even when you know you are qualified.

- Choose not to speak up in meetings or share your ideas due to fear of being judged or dismissed.

- Struggle to set boundaries or express your needs and desires, which leads to feelings of resentment and dissatisfaction.

- Neglect your own self-care and wellbeing.

- Decide not to ask for help.

- Withhold your ideas or suggestions when you know they will make a difference.

- Choose not to take on new opportunities, which leads to a feeling of stagnation.

- Feel you can't be vulnerable or that you need to know all the answers, so you don't step up and lead.

The advocate mindset: courage and intuition

Leaders with the mindset to advocate for themselves and others listen to the still, quiet voice of their intuition to make decisions. They have self-trust. These leaders back themselves and their ability to make decisions, sometimes without the advice of others, and they are comfortable backing themselves, even in the face of dissenting viewpoints. Leaders with this mindset go with their gut and place a high importance on having their own opinion or making their own decisions. When you are advocating for yourself, your family, or your team, you author your own decisions. You trust that you can recognize your own needs, values, beliefs, and discernments. You know your worth and you are not afraid to ask for what you need or want.

Making the power pivot

You know when you are advocating for yourself, and asking for and receiving what you deserve. When you are advocating, you are in your power zone. You are confident, assertive, and proactive. Here are some examples of what you might look like advocating in various contexts. You are:

- Comfortable saying "no" or managing disagreements and conflicts without overfocusing on pleasing others.

- Happy, when needed, to express a contrary opinion, play devil's advocate, or make recommendations that you know will not be popular.

- Listening to your needs and intuition, knowing that if you feel unfulfilled and uninspired, you can pivot to follow your passion in a more creative and purpose-driven field, role, or project.

- Setting clear boundaries with friends, family members, or colleagues who are not respecting your needs or values.

- Doing your research and knowing your worth, and, in turn, negotiating for a higher salary, more flexibility and/or autonomy, or better benefits.

- Pitching your idea, product, service, or the change you want to create in the world to decision makers, potential clients, investors, or influencers.

- Brokering connections, collaborations, and contracts, looking for a win-win for all involved and ensuring fair treatment and terms.

- Confidently calculating risk, and making decisions based on your intuition, your ability to read the context, and your experience.

- Listening to your intuition and declining a job offer that looks good on paper because you have assessed the "fit" (how the organization aligns with your values, ethics, preferred working arrangement, and so on) isn't right. You recognize that work culture matters to your productivity, confidence, and job satisfaction.

- Receiving conflicting advice from family and friends, yet trusting your own intuition when making decisions about your child's or children's education.

- Having an entrepreneurial spirit and a business idea, and subsequently doing your homework, gaining clarity on your vision and goals, pushing past your fear of failure and uncertainty, and taking the leap to start your business.

- Ending a toxic relationship or refusing to be bullied or harassed. After ignoring red flags or making excuses for the other person's behavior, you listen to your intuition and recognize that you deserve better, and you take action to end the relationship and prioritize your own wellbeing.

- Deciding to have a conversation with your micromanaging boss who constantly checks your work and insists on being involved in every decision. After reflection, and without defensiveness, you explain what you need (more autonomy and trust) and propose offering progress reports, which will meet your boss's needs.

In each of these examples, you are pivoting, calling on your courage and your inner wisdom to say "yes" or "no" to opportunities or challenges. You are making decisions by trusting yourself and referencing your own experience and strengths. You are in your power, and not afraid to speak up and advocate for yourself.

Power mindsets and reframes

This power pivot may require you to give up a damaging habit, emotional state, or distorted thinking pattern to gain what you want. Making this pivot will take practice and self-compassion. To make this power pivot, you will have to tap into your inner wisdom and begin to rely on your intuition to make decisions. This doesn't mean that you don't ask for feedback or consult with others. It requires you to build your bravery to reframe your thoughts and beliefs about yourself and others. With practice and focus, you can reframe yourself into a more powerful position to advocate for yourself or others. To begin to make your power pivot, identify if you have any of these habits or negative mindsets and start working today to reframe them.

Reframe Your Thoughts and Beliefs

DAMAGING PATTERNS OF THINKING
Discounting your inner wisdom

DESCRIPTION
Discounting is giving away your personal authority to decide for yourself, instead preferring others to make choices for you. Discounting could also include overaccommodating others by deferring to them for decision making or leadership.

REFRAME
Become aware of how you make decisions, and your inner dialogue and process.

Understand how your current patterns may be benefiting you or how they are costing you.

Understand your criteria for making decisions, including your values and priorities.

Begin to integrate your patterns, criteria, and actions with your values, purpose, and priorities.

Strengthen your intuition. You do this by noticing everything through your five senses, paying attention to your surroundings, and spending time in silence. Feel more, think less. Begin to rely on your senses and/or your gut to make decisions.

Start with small decisions and small risks. Build your confidence in accessing your intuition. Then move to more difficult situations that require you to reframe your relationship with intuition, self-trust, and courage.

Reframe your patterns, processes, and practices, and put yourself in the driver's seat.

DAMAGING PATTERNS OF THINKING
Judging and comparing

DESCRIPTION
You can judge yourself and judge others. Both are damaging.
Judging is a consistent pattern of criticizing, finding fault, and
making negative assessments of yourself, someone, or something.

REFRAME
Break this habit by remembering that everyone's experience and
preferences are unique, and listen and learn before forming an
opinion or sharing it.

Question the reasons for your reaction or judgment and understand why it bothers you.

Determine if the judgment reflects your own issues, insecurities, or
perfectionism. If so, learn to release or reframe.

Discover if your judgments reflect your emotions or fear. If so,
interrupt the pattern.

When you back yourself, you suspend your judgment of what
might happen and you assume the best in yourself, others, and
opportunities.

Don't let judgments hold you back from saying "yes" or "no" to
risks and opportunities.

Here are three resources that can help you release and reframe:

- *The Perfectionist's Guide to Losing Control: A Path to Peace and
  Power* by Katherine Morgan Schafler

- *Your Unstoppable Greatness: Break Free from Imposter Syndrome,
  Cultivate Your Agency, and Achieve Your Ultimate Career Goals* by
  Lisa Orbe-Austin and Richard Orbe-Austin

- *Judgment Detox: Release the Beliefs That Hold You Back from
  Living a Better Life* by Gabrielle Bernstein

DAMAGING PATTERNS OF THINKING
Filtering

DESCRIPTION
A pattern of thinking or habit of excluding the positive details of a situation or context. This pattern includes overfocusing on the negative details or aspects of situations.

REFRAME

You can break this habit by becoming aware of when you are filtering, how often, and the damage this is causing (stress, anxiety, fear, and so on).

Do you only see the negative aspects of yourself, others, or the situation at hand?

Does your filtering lead you to catastrophize or procrastinate?

Does your filtering lead you to assume the victim role too often?

Interrupt the pattern. Focus more often on the positive and what brings you gratitude instead.

Focus on releasing and reframing negative thought patterns that build your resistance to change or growth and diminish your confidence and courage.

DAMAGING PATTERNS OF THINKING
Catastrophizing

DESCRIPTION
Consistently expecting the worst to happen
Can be related to chronic worrying and anxiety

REFRAME
Focus on the outcome you want or intend and interrupt your negative thinking pattern by flipping your thinking to the best-case scenario or asking the question, "What could go right in this situation?"

Be curious about outcomes instead of expecting the worst-case scenario.

Celebrate the surprises when things turn out better than you expected.

If you suffer from constant worrying and anxiety, explore if there were critical incidents in your past that are driving your present or limiting your future. Helpful resources for this exploration include:

How to Do the Work: Recognize Your Patterns, Heal from Your Past, and Create Your Self by Nicole LePera

How to Meet Your Self: The Workbook for Self-Discovery by Nicole LePera

You're Not Broken: Break Free from Trauma and Reclaim Your Life by Sarah Woodhouse

DAMAGING PATTERNS OF THINKING
Establishing few or no boundaries

DESCRIPTION
Boundaries are essential to your health, happiness, and success because they contribute to defining who you are and how you will interact with others. In a work setting, boundaries help everyone involved understand who will be responsible for what, and the parameters or criteria for decision making.

Boundaries can be physical and emotional.

You may be experiencing a lack of boundaries if you are feeling angry, resentful, overwhelmed, or victimized.

REFRAME

Setting boundaries takes practice.

Learn the benefits of boundaries and how to set them.

Examples of when you need boundaries:

- You are afraid to say "no" to someone.
- You don't communicate your expectations.
- You don't speak up when you are mistreated.
- You make commitments you regret later.

Benefits of boundaries:

- Create clarity and define what you are responsible for.
- Create healthy limits.
- Provide physical and emotional safety.
- Establish priorities and consequences for non-action.
- Can improve relationships, health, and self-esteem.

How to set boundaries:

- Clarify what you need and want.
- Identify your options and then determine the boundary that is right for you.
- Implement the boundary you have chosen, test it, and tweak it if needed.

Boundaries are not selfish, and they are not demands, or ultimatums.

Boundaries are not mean or fixed, but part of two-way communication and negotiation.

Boundaries enable you and others to feel confident, respected, safe, and connected.

DAMAGING PATTERNS OF THINKING
Imposter syndrome

DESCRIPTION
Imposter syndrome is sometimes called perceived fraudulence.

You feel self-doubt and personal incompetence despite your accomplishments, experience, and education.

It can also include the feeling that you are an outsider, often triggered by your internal beliefs or by a setting that is not inclusive.

Trailblazers or pioneers in their fields often experience this negative belief pattern, which can be reframed with practice.

REFRAME
This can be viewed as a cycle that can be broken by identifying what critical incidents trigger your negative beliefs and behaviors (for example, overwork, self-sabotage).

You can learn mindsets, skills, and behaviors that can break the cycle of self-doubt.

Learn to build self-awareness and context-awareness.

Explore your internal beliefs and reframe those that lead to over-performing, which can lead to exhaustion and self-doubt.

Simple practices like better time and project management, and setting boundaries, can bring new perspectives about your positive contributions.

Learn how to receive compliments and practice internalizing positive feedback.

Actively silence your inner critic.

Practice perspective taking so that you can begin to regularly reframe self-doubt.

DAMAGING PATTERNS OF THINKING
Perfectionism

DESCRIPTION
Perfectionism is driven by a belief that you are unworthy and a fear of failure.

This trait causes you to set high goals and standards for yourself and others, and strive for flawless execution, which is unrealistic.

Elizabeth Scott, PhD, has found that this trait is developed via your upbringing and socialization, including social media, genetics, and trauma.

Perfectionism is linked to other disruptive patterns, such as over-activity, rumination, excessive attention to detail, and inflexibility.

REFRAME

Katherine Morgan Schafler, in her book *The Perfectionist's Guide to Losing Control: A Path to Peace and Power*, encourages you to swap language and perspectives to reframe. For example, for the trait of overactivity, swap energy management for time management.

For the trait of rumination, swap the viewpoint of "better" or "worse" for the viewpoint of "different."

Other reframes include setting realistic goals, trying new things that set you up to experience "failure," practicing mindfulness, and challenging your negative thoughts using self-compassion.

DAMAGING PATTERNS OF THINKING

Double standards

DESCRIPTION

This thought pattern is closely associated with perfectionism, whereby you hold yourself to a higher standard than you hold others.

REFRAME

Practice self-compassion.

Soften your self-talk.

Imagine how you would speak or provide feedback to a good friend or even a stranger.

Drop the comparison and perfectionism through reframing and practice.

Strategies for closing this power gap

It takes courage to be able to understand your context, needs, and goals and to put yourself first. It takes courage to speak your truth. It takes courage to solve problems, negotiate, and make decisions, or act despite your emotions, beliefs, and contextual dynamics. It also takes practice. As a leader, you will be called to speak and act on behalf of others, which is sometimes easier than taking a stand for yourself. Start to make your power pivots by learning to recognize your negative patterns of thinking and behaviors. Take small steps, practice, reflect, and celebrate the challenges you are taking on and the changes in your mindsets, patterns, and behaviors. Move on to close the gaps in the patterns that drain your power and have the highest impact on your life. In some cases, you may need to reach out to a coach for help with reading your context, reframing your mindsets, or learning new skills like setting boundaries. Based on what is driving your thought patterns, you may choose to change the context if it is the source of your negative patterns and triggering you to lose power.

For example, if you discover the power gap is due to a particular environment, there are steps that you can take. Consider these questions:

Is your family or work system enabling, and potentially benefiting from, your perfectionism, imposter syndrome, or other sabotaging patterns or behaviors like people pleasing, failure to establish boundaries, or overperformance?	Yes No
Are your co-workers constantly scheduling meetings in your calendar during your break times or on your non-working days?	Yes No
Is expressing your ideas or contrary opinions punished?	Yes No
Are you expected to be constantly "on call" for work outside of established working hours?	Yes No
Are there examples of not being included in meetings or projects that directly relate to your job description?	Yes No
Are there examples of not being provided the information that is needed for you to adequately perform your job?	Yes No
Is harassment, bullying, intentional or unintentional bias, inequities, or exclusionary behavior regularly tolerated among your superiors, peers, or subordinates?	Yes No

If you have answered "yes" to these questions, you may be in a toxic system where the power gap is being created because of factors outside of you. If you choose to stay in a toxic system, it will be difficult to make the internal changes necessary to close your personal power gap.

In this situation, you need to lean into your intuition and let your experience guide you. Weigh up the costs and benefits of staying in a toxic environment, and advocate for yourself by having the courage to move on if necessary.

Keys to courage for your power pivot

When you learn to move out of your comfort zone, to take risks, and put yourself first by backing yourself in the face of uncertainty, you make yourself the authority in your own life. There are some keys to closing this power gap and making the power pivot to advocate for yourself.

Be the authority in your own life

Are you looking for permission from others to think what you want to think, do what you want to do, or be who you want to be? Write your own permission slips. Give yourself permission! Your authority flows from your character, values, strengths, and authenticity. Find or develop your own personal authoritative style. Think of all the different ways you can embody your authority. Connect with your inner archetype or superhero that embodies your authority. Perhaps your archetype is that of a pioneer or founder—forging new pathways and establishing new ways of working. Or perhaps you are more of an artist or creative nurturer. Is your archetype a teacher, or mentor, who initiates actions courageously using intuition? Give yourself the permission to embody your strengths, superpowers, and convictions. Recognize your personal power. Cultivate your intuition. Your authority will grow with each courageous action. Watch how it inspires trust and respect in yourself and from others. Be inspired by it and others will be also. Giving yourself permission may require you to reframe your damaging patterns or kick your perfectionism or imposter syndrome to the curb.

Leave your comfort zone

Courage is a muscle that you can exercise. You can develop your own exercise routine, which should include identifying your fears and creating a strategy to move past them. It takes practice. Determine what causes your fear and proactively change your mental habits to remind yourself of times when you were afraid and acted anyway. Eventually your fear will call less often, and your courage will be available to you as an inner resource. Stop comparing yourself to others. This undermines your confidence. Stop focusing on your flaws. Recognize your strengths and courage, and learn how to use them in different situations. Make it a practice to step outside your comfort zone regularly. This will build your ability to call on your courage.

Learn the power of boundaries

Use your inner wisdom to say "yes" to opportunities and "no" to distractions that block you from achieving your goals. Boundaries have benefits. They improve your relationships, health, and self-esteem. They can provide physical and emotional safety, and ensure that you focus on what is important. If you lack consistent boundaries in your life, career, and business, you and others can be negatively affected. Here are examples of a lack of boundaries:

- You avoid saying "no" so that you don't disappoint people.

- You do not communicate your expectations, desires, or needs.

- You don't speak up when you are mistreated.

- You frequently feel angry, resentful, or overwhelmed.

- You aren't taking time to care for yourself.

- You don't have a strong sense of yourself, your values, or your goals.

- You blame yourself for things outside of your control.

The first step is identifying your boundaries and, step by step, practicing new mindsets and behaviors, reframing, and pivoting, until you establish boundaries that work for you and others.

Utilize your support team

Call on your "cheer squad" to recognize when your fears are holding you back and to help you consider your options and positive strategies. Find a mentor to help you broaden your ambitions and focus your goals and strategies. Secure a coach who can help you reframe and build new mindsets and strategies. Recruit sponsors who can open doors and be in the room when decisions are made that affect you. Leverage these influential resources to power up your courage and accelerate yourself forward.

POWERFUL QUESTIONS
THAT ACCELERATE YOU!

Before we move on, here are some questions I'd like you to think about:

1 In what areas of your life, career, or business are you waiting for others to give you permission to think, do, or be? Write your own permission slips to accelerate ahead. Include on your permission slip what permission you are granting yourself. What is the plan you are initiating? Include the date and your signature. Post it proudly to remind yourself you are the authority in your own life.

2 Get to know your inner superhero. Who is she? What does she stand for? What are some of her strategies? How can she help you achieve your goals?

3 What are the courageous acts you want to practice that will accelerate you toward your goals?

4 What boundaries do you want to set to create the change required to reach your goals?

Power affirmation: I am courageous!

CHAPTER 8

AMPLIFY

"One of the most calming and powerful
actions you can do to intervene in a stormy
world is to stand up and show your soul."

CLARISSA PINKOLA ESTÉS

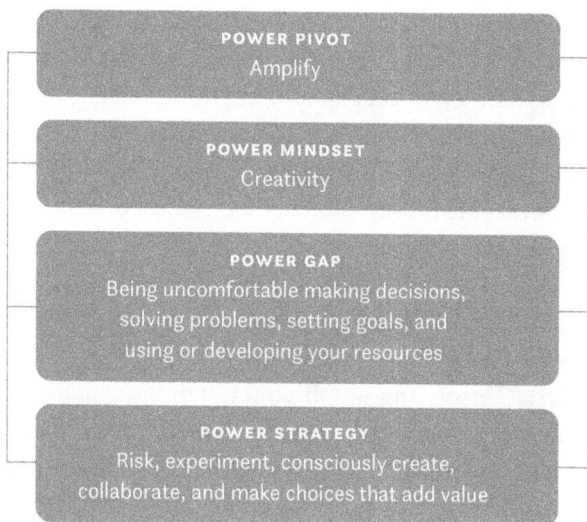

POWER PIVOT
Amplify

POWER MINDSET
Creativity

POWER GAP
Being uncomfortable making decisions,
solving problems, setting goals, and
using or developing your resources

POWER STRATEGY
Risk, experiment, consciously create,
collaborate, and make choices that add value

AMPLIFYING YOURSELF as a leader means getting comfortable with vulnerability, exposure, and standing out. Amplifying yourself is a process of moving from invisible to visible. For many women, myself included, this has been a challenge. Early in my career, it was uncomfortable for me to be "on stage" leading. I heard in my head the voices of the women who raised me. They had passed down their values and beliefs—from grandmother, to mother, to daughter. I heard, "Don't get too big for your britches, Jeri!" when I spoke confidently.

From an early age, I formed the limiting belief that leading from the front, taking a stand, and sharing my thoughts with others was a form of "stealing the spotlight." When I entered the workforce, the common wisdom for women seeking leadership success was to work hard, be well liked, remain in control of your emotions, don't take risks, don't complain, and don't ask for anything because you are just lucky to have found your place at the table. My mother's voice turned into the voice of my inner critic, saying to me, "Don't be aggressive or abrasive and be careful not to shine too bright."

As a result, leadership, self-promotion, standing out, and daring to be authentic never came easy for me. However, over the years, through a process of trial, error, and amplifying my unique qualities, I have developed a leadership style that reflects my values and personal truths and generates trust and engagement among those with whom I work.

I have found that using creativity as a tool and a process is essential when I am uncomfortable making decisions, solving problems, or setting goals. As a recovering perfectionist who is used to minimizing risks, overworking, and overperforming to create a false sense of control, substituting creativity for control is terrifying at first, but, once learned, becomes a freeing experience.

In this chapter, you will discover what a creativity power gap feels like and why it is essential that you close this power gap. You will learn about the amplify mindset, which enables your creativity, imagination, and innovation, ultimately helping you lead positive change in yourself and with others. You will learn about some of the damaging thought patterns and behaviors that create this power gap, and how to make a pivot to amplify your personal power.

What does a creativity power gap feel like?

When your creativity is blocked, you are not inspired, and you have very little enthusiasm or curiosity to generate new ideas or alternatives to meet the challenges or problems you face. You may feel cynical, tired, burnt out, like you're on autopilot, or you may suffer from low energy. You may feel stuck, empty, or depressed. You have lost your purpose, focus, and clarity, which means you cannot prioritize, or make decisions. You have lost connection to your inner resources and your go-to strategies for creatively getting results. You may have lost connection with your imagination, goals, or intended outcomes. You feel powerless to influence yourself or others.

How did you get here? You have been playing it safe—afraid to make mistakes or take chances. You have been avoiding learning, innovating, or changing. You have stopped experimenting, and it feels like you are "dead in the water" and there is no momentum. You may be holding your breath, feeling overwhelmed, or afraid to engage or collaborate for fear of losing control or—in contrast—using your power to make choices that affect other people. You may see yourself as lost or not knowing where to start, where to go, or what to do to regain your "mojo." You may be experiencing your fear and feel it eating at you in the pit of your stomach, triggered by the notion that you don't want to take up space, step up, or stand out. Suddenly you realize that you have stopped believing in yourself or others. If you are experiencing any of these thoughts, feelings, or sensations, your power is leaking.

WHAT DO WOMEN EXPERIENCING THIS POWER GAP OFTEN SAY?

"I see the women around me making big career moves and I think, 'It is all right for you,' but my situation is different—I just can't imagine myself doing that or that working here."

"How do these women do that? I am smarter than them—they just must be lucky!"

"I have been around here a long time and I have seen it all. The ideas from this new team are never going to work here."

"I don't have time to be creative. I am so busy just doing business as usual."

"I never share my ideas anymore in that forum. Why bother?"

What are some examples of how you leak your power? Being uncomfortable to make decisions, solve problems, or use your internal resources is a power gap requiring you to amplify your personal power and influence others. When you are experiencing this power gap, you struggle to prioritize, delegate, ideate, innovate, and influence others. Here are some examples of when you know you have a power gap:

- You feel you've lost your creative "spark" and find it difficult to solve problems or make decisions. Or you start the creative process, and you struggle to complete the project or get the results you desire.

- You struggle to prioritize your tasks and responsibilities at work, leading to a lack of productivity or effectiveness.

- You hear yourself saying "yes" to every opportunity that comes your way, even if it means sacrificing your health and wellbeing, because you haven't created boundaries.

- You find it difficult to delegate tasks because you don't trust others to do the job well or because you feel like you should be able to handle things yourself—leading to feelings of burnout or a lack of work-life balance.

- You need to control every aspect of your team's work because you don't trust them to do a good job, which leads to you being overwhelmed and your team feeling demotivated and disempowered.

- Although you have great ideas and insights, you struggle to effectively communicate them to others, or to get others on board with your vision, which limits your ability to lead or create impact.

- You are afraid to speak up in meetings to share your ideas even when you know your ideas will be valuable.

- You don't negotiate your salary during your job offer, or you don't ask for that project that will give you the skills and experience required for your next role, or you fail to ask for that raise or promotion.

- You consistently take on too much responsibility without a pathway to delegate or a connection to the resources required.

- You stay in a role too long because you fear failure, or you don't feel qualified for the roles you really desire.

The amplify mindset: creativity, imagination, and innovation

Leaders who use their personal power with comfort are creative and collaborative when seizing opportunities. They easily make decisions using their imagination and by innovating. They are comfortable in their personal authority and with their authority over decisions, people, priorities, and budgets. They enjoy overseeing their life, career, and business, and appreciate discipline, responsibility, and hierarchy—often leveraging their position to achieve goals. They influence people around them. If you are uncomfortable with your personal power, you could be reluctant to take responsibility or act from your position of authority, which results in reduced levels of influence where and when it counts. If you can use your imagination, you can be creative and think outside the box to reach your greatest desires. Are you ready to conceive of what you need to create and reach your goals?

Making the power pivot

To amplify your personal power, voice, and presence to influence yourself and others, you must be:

- Comfortable making decisions, solving problems, setting goals, and using the resources around you.

- Willing to move out of your comfort zone to take risks, experiment, consciously create, collaborate, and make choices that add value.

- Actively working to increase the sound, color, brightness, and experience of your imagination, and deepening your practice of innovation.

- Consistently gathering new experiences, practices, and resources that will help you boost and pivot your mindset for creativity.

Power mindsets and reframes

Making this pivot means that you must take a risk, experiment, learn, and make different choices. The power strategy here is to lean into experimentation and improvisation, creating collaboratively, and making choices that add value.

If you are experiencing a power gap at this step, explore what is causing the gap or block in creativity, imagination, or innovation. Do you feel uncomfortable connecting with your talents, skills, and vision to make decisions, create solutions, or leverage your resources? Are you stressed, burnt out, or filled with self-doubt because you have set unattainable goals or chosen unsustainable strategies? Do you need to tune up your routine to better align with your motivations around change? Are you stuck in a cycle of busyness that leads you to resent or reject learning something new? Is there something missing in the culture or the team that is keeping creativity from thriving? Perhaps there is an opportunity to rethink your strategies, routine, or context to get unstuck, prioritize creativity, and support innovation. Determine where you are stuck, and then shift your mindset and reframe any patterns of thinking that are blocking you.

It is important to know that amplifying yourself—putting yourself out there, whether it is stepping up to lead for the first time, taking the stage to present your ideas, expressing a contrary view, influencing others to change, moving toward goals, raising your leadership profile, actively building your leadership brand, or starting up a new product line or company—means you will be on an emotional journey.

The journey will be fraught with emotions and thinking patterns that you will need to navigate. Howard Love, in his book, *The Start-Up J Curve: The Six Steps to Entrepreneurial Success*, describes both the emotional journey startup founders take when bringing their ideas to the market and the stages they experience in their businesses. These stages are create, release, morph, model, scale, and harvest. I have adapted Love's concepts for the startup or innovation journey and have applied it to the journey we take for personal transformation and change.

To amplify your personal power, you must take a risk, knowing that you will be emotionally exposed and vulnerable. As you take the leap and create, you must release expectations of perfection. You don't have to have all the answers before you start. Mistakes will happen. Become comfortable in jumping in and learning from "failure." Release your need to structure and overplan, and, instead, act and then incrementally morph or make changes as you move ahead. Become comfortable in collaborating and creating with those around you. Benchmark how others you admire are creating a future they desire. Model your mindsets and actions based on people you see around you who are gaining momentum and getting results. And when it is appropriate, don't be afraid to pioneer new pathways. When you see things are working, continue to amplify your results by scaling up your practices in a way that will be repeatable and sustainable for you and others. Embody the changes and harvest the results while celebrating your wins along the way.

As you become more comfortable with the stages, you will also become more comfortable with the creative process. You will find your own power zone, and build your own power toolkit, by collecting the tools and tips that work for you and using them regularly to power up your clarity, confidence, courage, and creativity for growth. You will also be more self-aware, knowing how to effectively manage yourself along the pathway and "growth hack" yourself to success. This term, used by startup founders, refers to the strategies you deploy for momentum and growth.

Your Change Curve

Consider a change that you are implementing in your life, career, or business. What is your experience of leading this change? What kind of emotions have you experienced recently? You can create momentum in your life, career, or business by embodying your learning curve and seeing it as your pathway to creating the change you desire. When you embody these stages, you will see that you may have to reframe your relationship with your imagination, the creative process, and the context and cultures that support innovation. This reframing process includes reframing any of the damaging patterns of thinking that create power gaps.

Take a moment to determine whether you have any of these thinking patterns that could be creating a gap in your creativity, so you can reframe them and make a power pivot.

Reframe Your Thoughts and Beliefs

DAMAGING PATTERNS OF THINKING
Playing small and seeking invisibility

DESCRIPTION
When you play small, you are holding your gifts within rather than sharing them with the world.

When you play small or strive to be invisible, you are holding back and being less than authentic, and killing your passion and inspiration.

This may be a conscious or unconscious pattern, motivated by your fears or insecurities. You may have adopted this unconscious and damaging pattern at a young age to stay safe, or later in life when you lived or worked in a hostile or toxic environment.

You may be hiding out if you are uncomfortable planning, budgeting, prioritizing, delegating, or having responsibility and authority over others.

Are you comfortable being invisible? Or do you wait to be "asked" for your opinion when you know your ideas can make a difference?

Are you afraid to showcase your talent? Are you waiting to be given a seat at the table?

Explore what unconscious pattern you may have adopted to keep you from being responsible or for leading.

Are you more comfortable conforming?

Is it easier to be helpless?

Do you get lost in busyness instead of stepping up and leading or seizing opportunities that could bring you what you want?

REFRAME

Begin honoring your passions, needs, boundaries, and accomplishments. Celebrate them!

Get in touch with your imagination and visualize what you really want. Make a vision board.

Remind yourself of your vision regularly. Remember to amplify yourself and your vision.

This will require you to dig deep and understand what is causing your fears and insecurities, and then reframing or clearing your fears.

Check to see if your feelings of vulnerability are coming from a fear of failure, a fear of losing people, a fear of offending others, a fear of embarrassing yourself, or a fear of change.

Get to the bottom of what is triggering you and keeping you small and invisible. Work with a coach to reframe your beliefs, disrupt yourself, or change your context—you may be triggered by your life or work culture.

Society often expects women to be weak, quiet, and small—these are feminine virtues, right? As a child, were you told that you were being "too much?" Give yourself permission to come out of the shadows.

Practice getting out of your comfort zone and taking risks by making risk taking or creativity fun!

If you have always been quiet, take a singing class or join a choir and "roar!"

Track every time you face your fear and create or innovate despite your fears. Celebrate and reward yourself.

DAMAGING PATTERNS OF THINKING
Not knowing your risk appetite

DESCRIPTION

Your risk appetite is the amount of risk that you are willing to take in various situations, or the risk appetite in your context or organization. Your risk appetite reflects your upbringing, culture, and history.

You can learn to assess and flex your risk appetite or risk mindset.

You can learn to become more comfortable with ambiguity or uncertainty.

This may mean that you learn to consciously take on risk until you feel more comfortable with the stages of creativity.

The key is to be aware of yourself, your needs, and the situation, context, or system you are in and to align your appetite appropriately.

REFRAME

The reframe here is to become aware of how often you stay in your comfort zone. Are you on autopilot? Is this an opportunity to stretch and try new things because there is very little risk—aside from being uncomfortable with your vulnerability? Or is the situation calling for you to look before you leap?

Be inspired by your imagination. Listen to your intuition. Innovate when it makes sense. Be conscious and choose.

Learning to assess, reframe, and choose your appetite to fit the situation is crucial for personal growth.

DAMAGING PATTERNS OF THINKING
Fearing failure

DESCRIPTION

The fear of failure can produce emotional and behavioral symptoms such as anxiety, avoidance, feelings of loss of control, helplessness, or powerlessness.

Do you believe that you won't be able to achieve—that you don't have what it takes?

Do you underestimate your own abilities and avoid feelings of being let down?

Do you worry you will disappoint others?

Fearing failure can impact your self-esteem and motivation. It is a form of self-sabotage and can come from a fear of shame, embarrassment, and worthlessness.

REFRAME

Practice self-compassion.

Recognize that this is a normal feeling and remind yourself that failure is part of learning and part of any change process.

Embrace learning from your mistakes.

Look more deeply at your fears. Become curious and experimental and adopt a beginner's mindset as you become open to learning from your mistakes.

Focus on the present.

Avoid personalizing or overgeneralizing failures.

Begin to calculate the cost of non-action and to quantify the benefits of acting.

DAMAGING PATTERNS OF THINKING
Not having a wellbeing or self-care routine

DESCRIPTION
Wellbeing is an experience of health, happiness, and prosperity.

Wellbeing comes from a routine of good mental and physical health, and includes a sense of life satisfaction, meaning or purpose, and the ability to manage stress.

Your personal power and success strategy depend on you developing a wellbeing routine and schedule that includes healthy habits (meals, movement, sleep, and so on).

REFRAME
This reframe is highly personal.

Begin with awareness of what is missing in your mindset and in your life that could make you feel more clear, confident, courageous, creative, and able to take on challenges and change.

Do you see self-care as overindulgent?

Or perhaps you don't know what self-care means; it feels to you like the latest fad.

The World Health Organization defines self-care as "the ability of individuals, families and communities to promote health, prevent disease, [and] maintain health … with or without the support of a health worker."

Don't use overwork, time pressures, or burnout as your primary strategy for success. Look at the science and develop a daily routine that supports you and your goals.

Strategies for closing this power gap

To raise your personal power to create and innovate, you must be comfortable with nurturing your ideas, and imagining what it will take to give birth to them. This means being comfortable prioritizing, solving problems, making decisions (often with incomplete information), setting goals, gathering resources, and taking risks to turn your goals into reality. Learn the stages of creativity and change. The creative process begins with gathering information about the project and identifying sources of inspiration. Then you let the information sink in and take root in your subconscious. After sowing these seeds, your insights will grow and often you will have a breakthrough idea, solution, or insight. Next you assess the desirability, feasibility, and viability of your ideas. Finally, you refine your ideas, often validating and refining by gathering feedback from others or experimenting.

To master innovation and change, you must be comfortable with, and capable of, making a business case for your ideas and following the money, results, and impact. Part of the creative process is being comfortable with expressing yourself persuasively with a sense of presence. Innovation involves inspiring and influencing yourself and others while also involving others in the creative process. Making this power pivot will call you to be more comfortable self-promoting, pitching your ideas, collaborating with people, and leveraging the dynamics in your context to create your intended results.

Keys to creativity for your power pivot

There are some keys to closing this power gap and making the power pivot to amplify yourself.

Remove your cloak of invisibility
Self-promotion can be incredibly uncomfortable. You may have been raised to believe that "big noting" yourself was unattractive. Many women don't

want to draw attention to themselves or want to wait for credit to find them. Are you still waiting? Are you more comfortable being invisible? What is that costing you? Know your strengths, and be able to describe your expertise, the results you deliver, the problems that you solve, and the impact that creates for others. Take actions today to amplify your voice, presence, or power to be creative and reach your goals. Amy Cuddy, in her book *Presence: Bringing Your Boldest Self to Your Biggest Challenges*, teaches that presence can be learned, and how tiny tweaks and hacks lead to big changes. Amanda Blesing outlines a formula for stepping out of the shadows in her books *Step Up, Speak Out, Take Charge* and *Invisible to Invincible*.

Make friends with "fast failure"

Take risks to build your creativity muscles. Sometimes you will fail. It is in the failure that you learn. It is in the discomfort that you develop your strengths, resilience, and the knowledge that you can meet any challenge. "Fast failure" is a strategy to take on problem solving that focuses on learning from experimentation. Recognize that failure is part of the pursuit of your goals. It is a badge of honor. Learn the valuable lessons that come from taking the risk. You cannot imagine, create, or innovate if you do not take risks. Your goal should not be perfection. Learn to celebrate your failures and your creativity as you celebrate your wins.

Build your capacity for empathy

The process of creativity produces new and valuable products, services, and perspectives. Empathy is a form of perspective taking, and a skill that leaders need, and is critical to achieving entrepreneurial and innovation goals. Empathy can enhance your creativity as you begin to see things from different angles, focus on thoughts, emotions, and your audience, and as you challenge your assumptions. Considering other people's perspectives and caring about their needs enhances creativity, problem solving, and decision making.

Aleksandr Litvinov, in conducting research on empathy with myself, Anne Gardner, and Sojen Pradhan, has found that empathy and perspective taking can be learned. Kirstin Ferguson, in her book *Head and Heart: The Art of Modern Leadership*, frames a new leadership model in which empathy is one of eight critical leadership attributes, pointing out that empathy enables you to stay in deep connection to collaborate, create, and lead from the center, resulting in better outcomes for all involved.

POWERFUL QUESTIONS
THAT ACCELERATE YOU!

Before we move on, here are some questions I'd like you to think about:

1. In what area of your life, career, or business do you "play small," hold yourself back, or fail to use your voice or personal power? What is that choice costing you?

2. What area of your life, career, or business do you want to amplify? What strategies will you use to create a power pivot? What is a step you can take today to amplify yourself?

3. Do you value the diversity of your abilities, experiences, and perspectives, and those of others? How can you actively seek to incorporate different perspectives into your decision making and collaborations?

4. Does the culture that surrounds you contribute to your experience of being invisible? Do you feel overlooked when you want to be seen, or are you being bypassed or not listened to? If so, how can you close the power gap?

Power affirmation: I am creative, and I can create a life, career, and business that doesn't exist today.

CHAPTER 9

ADVANCE

"Every great dream begins with a dreamer.
Always remember, you have within you the
strength, the patience, and the passion
to reach for the stars to change the world."

HARRIET TUBMAN

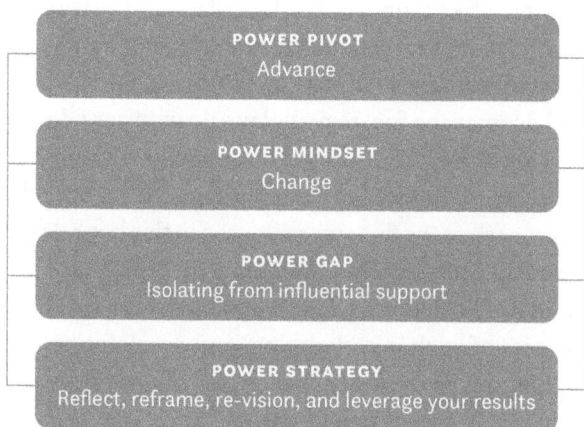

POWER PIVOT
Advance

POWER MINDSET
Change

POWER GAP
Isolating from influential support

POWER STRATEGY
Reflect, reframe, re-vision, and leverage your results

T HAS TAKEN me a long time to learn how to imagine the change I wanted to create in my life, and how to advance myself toward my goals, despite adversity. I am still working on embodying the change I want to see in my world.

Through my research, and my work with leaders and entrepreneurs, I estimate that about eighty per cent of your success in advancing toward your goals is related to your mindset. You may have experienced success, but it is rare that when you want to make a change in your life, career, or business that you experience success daily. I found that to be true for me. There have been moments in my life and career when I started moving toward a goal and then I struggled. I would begin to feel a bit stuck, and I would begin to question myself. How did I get here and what is the next step that will get me back on track?

Now, after many trials and tribulations, I've learned that in order to sustain changes that I put in place, I need to reconnect with my inspiring vision. This clarity becomes the fuel to power me up with confidence and gives me the courage to consciously make better choices. Today, I still am finding creative ways to enact each of the five steps outlined in this book. I continue to discover how to advance myself toward my goals, and celebrate where I am and who I am. This process of evolving, changing, and accelerating is a continuous process. My change curve is an emotional journey, and it has taught me resilience, grit, and the importance of self-awareness as a daily practice.

In this chapter, you will learn what it looks, sounds, and feels like to embody change in your life, career, and business. You will discover the advance mindsets, which relate to how you manage the change process and the components of change as you make small and big changes in your life. You will discover the importance of celebrating change, as well as your results and impact. You will also discover the power strategies for closing this power gap. I will give you the keys to leading change for your power pivot and the questions you must ask yourself.

What does a change power gap feel like?

Women (and men) experience this power gap when they feel invisible and unrecognized for their contributions, aren't supported by their supervisors, or are experiencing the effects of the toxic culture they're in. There are factors within your workplace that can drive feelings of isolation. When women don't experience an equal playing field, don't feel included, or come up against barriers to advancement, this creates an external power gap.

Women can also experience internal barriers to achieving a sense of personal advancement. You can experience this power gap internally when you try to advance alone without enrolling career allies, mentors, or sponsors. As a result, you may begin to feel a sense of frustration or resignation. You can feel this power gap when you put off what is most important to you or even the simplest pleasure, believing that overwork is a sustainable strategy. You can feel a lack of advancement if you don't find ways to embrace, embody, or celebrate the progress you have made. You can experience this gap if you make changes that are unsustainable or, in your busyness, you don't reflect on and integrate what you have learned into your routine. You can feel the power gap as you struggle to understand the change process, become overwhelmed and lost in the emotional change journey, or don't see the need and benefits of change. Experiences like these make you vulnerable to not initiating the change that will deliver the results you want or could cause you to abandon yourself and the process at the first obstacle, seeing you revert to old and damaging habits, processes, or mindsets.

While it is natural for you to feel fear in amplifying yourself and stepping up to lead, when you do take the step to advance yourself you must push through the fear, leverage your courage, and creatively meet each challenge. As you step up and stand out as a leader, you must overcome the internal power gap of being isolated from influential support (allies, supporters, mentors, coaches, career sponsors, and partners) who can collaborate with you to enable change.

Women describe this power gap as feeling disheartened, defeated, exhausted, stuck, jaded, depleted, and powerless.

WHAT DO WOMEN EXPERIENCING THIS POWER GAP OFTEN SAY?

"I am exhausted and dead; I live for the weekends."

"I am tired of playing politics."

"At this point, I just keep my head down."

"I feel trapped and stuck. I have tried to step up, but it's just too hard here."

"Why have a vision for change when this work culture doesn't support innovation?"

"I have tried to fight the 'good fight.' Now I leave my purpose at the door and work here for the paycheck."

What are some examples of how you leak your power? When you don't embrace your personal ability to lead change, you may have disconnected from the inner resources and strengths that enable you to thrive and adapt. If you have made the decision not to change because you have a fixed mindset, you have unplugged your connection with your power resource. If you don't see the benefit of change, you may not have fully explored your vision for yourself and the future to truly understand what you may gain from change. You may not be fulfilling your desires, utilizing your talents, or feeling connected to the emotions and personal truths that can guide you through change.

The inner container that holds your personal power may be leaking because you haven't put any boundaries in place. When your container is strong, you can manage and restore your energy, enhance your resilience, and maintain your ability to face obstacles and setbacks that come with change and leadership. Whether you are leading change for yourself or with others inside your family, community, or organization, it is important to emotionally connect within and with those who are going to be a part of the change. Here are some examples of how you leak your power:

- You aren't fully recognizing, experiencing, and managing your emotions to raise your energy to inspire yourself and others.

- You have lost touch with the purpose that fuels your energy and resilience.

- You don't set clear boundaries with your colleagues or clients and end up feeling overwhelmed and overworked.

- You procrastinate or fail to initiate opportunities, or fail to communicate what you need.

- You resist change or new ideas, or may struggle to see the big picture, or to think laterally or creatively, leaving you feeling stagnant.

- You don't prioritize self-care or take time for your-self and end up feeling burnt out and exhausted.

- You don't hold yourself accountable or manage your focus.

- You initiate too much change at one time, or do not monitor or measure results.

- You fail to speak out against poor, inappropriate, unethical, or unjust behavior that you know is wrong.

- You haven't developed a positive relationship to change, creating results and impact, or you haven't fully integrated your learning into your body or habits, or you have yet to develop your knowledge about leading the change process.

When a woman appreciates her abilities, progress, ambition, and impact, she exudes confidence, self-assurance, and a positive attitude toward herself and her achievements. She recognizes her strengths and is aware of her limitations. However, instead of dwelling on her weaknesses, she uses them as opportunities for growth and improvement. She is not afraid to take risks or try new things because she knows that her past successes and failures have prepared her for future challenges. When a woman is focused on advancing herself and others around her, she leverages her vision, results, and resources to reach her goals. She recruits a support team of role models, mentors, coaches, allies, partners, and sponsors. She is proud of her accomplishments and recognizes the value that she brings to her personal and professional life. She is comfortable with, and capable of, standing up and standing out to tell her story of impact. This appreciation of herself and her abilities allows her to operate at her highest level of personal power, leading to further success and fulfillment in all areas of her life.

The advance mindset: embracing and celebrating change and impact

Leaders who reflect, reframe, re-vision, and leverage their internal and external resources for the results they desire take radical action for impact. These leaders are persistent. They fuel their vision because it drives them. When you are using this mindset, you are willing to go for it—to make mistakes and figure it out along the way to overcome the challenges, solve the problems, and make a difference. Leaders who are focused on impact measure their progress toward goals, are patient and reflective, are driven by achievement, and enjoy leading or making change. The process of covering new ground toward the goal inspires them and keeps them moving forward. Their goals and their results are top of mind, and they are comfortable sharing with others their story of impact, for they know that describing the journey and the progress inspires not only themselves but others. These leaders take the time to fully embody and embrace the change they have created and embed the changes to ensure their sustainability and momentum for the next opportunity.

This power strategy also relates to your affinity and attitudes toward money, finance, and the achievement of goals. What is your relationship to change and money? Explore this and you'll have a better understanding of how you can close the power gap and accelerate forward.

Your mindsets matter. Are you motivated to stick with the status quo and keep things the same?

Are you motivated to make incremental improvements in your life, in your career, or in the workplace? This focus on evolutionary change is critical for embedding new behaviors or achieving long-term results.

Are you motivated to start projects from scratch and take paths that do not yet exist? You may be motivated to disrupt the status quo, spot differences, and look at things from unique perspectives, or create radical change, which is linked to creativity, entrepreneurship, and innovation. You may notice that you are among the early adopters, if not leading the way.

In short, is your motivation for sameness, evolution, or difference enabling you or holding you back from creating the change you want to make in your life, career, or business? You can shift your mindset to supercharge your momentum, results, and impact.

Making the power pivot

To raise your personal power to advance yourself and others, you must be comfortable with monitoring the evolution of changes you are creating so that you can build on them to create momentum and results. This pivot is about determining if the change you have created is desirable, feasible, scalable, and sustainable. In other words, what will it take to sustain change and make it a personal habit or integrate it into your life, career, or business?

Your goal with this step is to embody the change with new habits and processes that get results consistently and become second nature. When you involve others in the change journey, you will advance the change best by being able to mark and celebrate the milestones and continue to inspire further change by reinforcing the reason for change and its value and impact. It is a continual process of reflecting and reframing, with a focus on the value and the impact that you are creating for yourself and others. You will find that continuing to communicate success with a focus on impact will be the inspiration that fuels the next wave of change required—powering up yourself and others for your future goals and challenges.

Determine what is keeping you from embracing the change that is needed. Perhaps you know it is important to change, but experience resistance to the change within yourself or from others around you. What is standing in the way? Determine where you are stuck, and then shift your mindset and reframe any patterns of thinking that are keeping you from advancing or preventing others from appreciating your evolution, value proposition, and impact in the world.

Steps to enhance your evolution:

- Take the time to understand your strengths, weaknesses, motivations, and leadership and communication styles to become more aware of your tendencies and adjust your self-beliefs and behaviors if necessary.

- Seek and provide constructive feedback, challenge yourself and those around you to improve, collect information, track results, and celebrate improvements in your own evolution and in the change involving others.

- Establish practices that are transparent, consistent, and reliable and make those around you feel included, engaged, and safe to take risks, speak up, and collaborate—helping all involved to make informed decisions and to take ownership of their work.

- Take proactive steps to address bias, promote diversity, and create opportunities for all collaborators to succeed.

- Embody your values and the behaviors that you want to develop in others, such as creativity, collaboration, innovation, and connectedness.

Steps to develop your value proposition:

- Visualize the arc of your life, career, and business aspirations, as well as the ways you want to develop and the transformation you want to create.

- Identify the problems you want to solve, the benefits you want to provide with your leadership, and the value you want to offer to those around you.

- Benchmark the leaders around you and differentiate yourself as a leader, focusing on your unique value and intended outcomes.

- Develop your personal brand by making your value proposition clear and compelling. Collect information about what is important to your customers and stakeholders, as well as information about your results, sharing what they can expect from your leadership in benefit-driven language.

- Use your value proposition as a compass to help make decisions, set priorities, and achieve goals.

Steps to maximize your impact:

- Choose work aligned to your passion.

- Learn to initiate quickly and consistently; avoid overplanning and procrastination, and pivot when necessary.

- Rethink your relationship with risk by developing your growth mindset, as discussed in Chapter 2.

- Highlight your competence and results by creating a vision of what success looks like for you and developing and delivering a plan for that vision.

- Stay humble. Few people are motivated or inspired by arrogant, boastful leaders. However, leaders do need to communicate progress and inspire themselves and others with factual updates. Develop a technique that works for you to track your evolution and progress toward your goals.

Power mindsets and reframes

This power pivot will require you to embrace change in yourself and learn to master the change process for yourself and others. Begin by asking yourself if you are ready for the change. Consider, too, those involved in the change, as well as the culture, environment, or context that will support the change. Assess your change readiness. You may have to enlist the support of influential others to advance the change. You may have to add or change your mindsets (or the mindsets of others) to make this pivot. You may have to give up damaging habits, emotional states, or distorted thinking patterns to gain what you want. With practice and focus, you can reframe yourself, build your change mastery, and achieve results.

You may need to describe your results in the ways that matter to yourself and others, and to highlight the impact you and others are making. If you aren't celebrating the changes you are making, put on your party hat. If you aren't sure what is holding you back, explore why the change is needed, what you will gain from the change, and what might be blocking you. Identify any mindsets that are causing you to procrastinate or resist change, or that are limiting your leadership and impact. Explore if your current strategies for change are fully considering the context for the change and the perspectives of others involved in leading the change. Determine if your thoughts, beliefs, and approaches to change are slowing you from advancing and sustaining the change that you want. If you are experiencing any of these obstacles to leading change, you can start working today to reframe them.

Reframe Your Thoughts and Beliefs

DAMAGING PATTERNS OF THINKING
Fear or negative attitudes about money

DESCRIPTION
Everyone has a personal relationship with money.

Money, including managing budgets and making financial decisions, can bring out an array of emotions (guilt, envy, fear, shame).

From your upbringing and personal experiences, you have developed thinking patterns, beliefs, and emotions about money.

Money coach Kate Bradley has defined five money mindsets:

1 The sufferer believes they can't make decisions about money and feels helpless or powerless regarding money.

2 The survivor has had past experiences with money that hinder their relationship with money, including financial planning, and spending money.

3 The passenger accepts the status quo, doesn't maximize earning capacity, doesn't innovate financially, or doesn't change their money habits until they see others making positive gains.

4 The driver works hard for her money, engages in "side hustles" and is modestly successful, but can get overwhelmed from juggling multiple goals and priorities.

5 The thriver is comfortable developing multiple revenue streams, educates herself, adds new strategies when needed, and has an abundance mindset.

According to regular surveys conducted by the American Psychological Association, money is a leading stress trigger.

In contrast, my own research (into patterns of women's career management, conducted with my colleagues Tania Machet and Michelle Duval) shows women *don't* rank money as a key driver in their decision making when selecting roles, career paths, or projects.

Know your values, attitudes, and beliefs around money to determine whether you want to make a pivot in mindset.

REFRAME

Pay attention to your thoughts, feelings, and actions related to money.

You can reframe or shift your money mindset if you choose.

Begin to understand your mindset and money story.

Fully unpack what is driving you when it comes to money.

If this is a mindset you want to change, a coach can help you.

You may not seek to be wealthy, but you can develop new knowledge and skills related to money.

To rise in organizations or to start up your own business, you must develop a money mindset and skills related to optimizing systems, budgeting, profitability, and cash flow management.

A commercial mindset is a trait that many employers are seeking and is essential in leadership roles and for successful startup and scaleup founders.

DAMAGING PATTERNS OF THINKING

Making big changes too often and not embedding
the results using maintenance goals

DESCRIPTION

When your mindset is focused on big change, you are motivated by revolutionary or radical pivots.

People who are motivated by big change are focused on finding what is missing in their life, career, or business situation.

Having the right mindset for radical change, and focusing on creating a difference, is essential when it comes to having the energy and desire to start things from scratch or forge a path that does not yet exist.

The higher the motivation, the more of a pioneer you are. This may be disruptive if you do not match this with mindsets and strategies for embedding the change, maintaining the results, continuing the momentum, or bringing others along the change journey who are less motivated.

REFRAME
Take a moment to balance decision making with reflection on both the positives and challenges of big change.

The adage "Look before you leap" doesn't imply that you should not leap, but to fully consider the long-term pathway to change, including the context and other factors in your environment that will support or sabotage your change strategies.

Reframe by questioning whether you are making too many changes at once. If so, focus on one change at a time.

You can reframe by asking yourself, "Am I driving too much change for too long?"

Are you and those you are leading worn out and lacking the energy required for more or sustainable change?

You can reframe by considering a more gradual change process that can offer consistency and sustainability.

This reframe is also necessary as entrepreneurs move out of startup mode and into scaleup mode, where efficiencies, consistent business models, and processes are necessary to create growth and profitability.

DAMAGING PATTERNS OF THINKING
Not knowing or considering the change mindsets of others

DESCRIPTION
Each person has three dimensions to their motivations for change: 1) no change mindset, 2) small/slow change mindset, and 3) fast/big change mindset.

Knowing other people's mindsets for change can help you get them on board or help you develop strategies that pace the change you are leading.

REFRAME
Reframe your strategies by taking perspective, understanding the change mindsets of others, and assessing your organization's cultural readiness to change before you initiate change.

Begin to understand the role of unintentional bias in our society and organizations.

Researchers have studied how this bias affects women, particularly with regard to their effectiveness in leading and communicating, and how they are seen and heard by others who are a part of any change process.

Knowing the impact of bias and culture on the change process is important, from creating the vision for change to implementing creatively and innovatively.

These contexts and biases affect the change process and the strategies required to advance yourself and your ideas in the workplace and the marketplace.

Reframe by learning how others process information about change and how others are convinced that change is required.

DAMAGING PATTERNS OF THINKING

Not knowing how others can be influenced by leadership styles, communication styles, or the degree to which you and others focus on goals or problems

DESCRIPTION

Your preferences related to leadership style can create momentum or slow your momentum toward change.

Your preferences or mindsets for focusing on goals rather than solving problems as a strategy for change must be considered when you catalyze change.

Does it inspire you or others to achieve a goal or anticipate and solve problems to create the change? When you craft your change strategy, align the roles, tasks, milestones, and storytelling with what motivates you and others.

Are you and others motivated by achievement? Some people are not inspired to achieve goals, particularly if they are goals they didn't help create.

Are you or others influenced to change by a vision and the big picture? Or, rather, by understanding the details of the next steps of the change?

Are you influenced by, or do you influence others by, building affiliation and collaboration in the change process?

Do you prefer to use your personal and formal authority to direct change? Do those involved in the change process prefer to be led by traditional top-down leadership styles?

Do you and others share your preferences for focusing on the past or future when innovating?

Do you and others share your preferences regarding decision making, sharing responsibility, or communicating? If you don't share perspectives, you may be working at odds with each other.

Learn what motivates you and others involved in the change process, and adjust your strategies to influence yourself and others to advance together.

REFRAME

Reframe by knowing your mindsets and preferences, and those of others.

Reframe by being adaptable; choose the leadership and communication styles that will resonate.

If the change you are leading involves others, reframe by understanding if the change is your solo responsibility or requires shared responsibility, and consider how others make decisions, including what they need to make decisions.

DAMAGING PATTERNS OF THINKING
Not measuring, managing, or celebrating change or growth

DESCRIPTION
Do you have a measurement mindset?

Are you establishing specific goals that are measurable, attainable, relevant, and time-bound?

When you are experimenting and initiating change, you must measure the results to evaluate and adjust your strategies.

To fuel your momentum, celebrating even the smallest changes is important.

When you are making personal changes, you need to remind yourself of what you have won, what you have learned, and how you have grown. Otherwise, you may just lose sight of your progress.

REFRAME
You can reframe how you measure, manage, and celebrate change.

One example of reframing is increasing your level of interest in, and your capacity to work with, money, finance, and other measures of success.

Research indicates that women tend to be motivated by a wide variety of success measures, which may not put money at the top of the list.

Having an appreciation of money, capabilities in managing money, and experience in measuring and monitoring key metrics for success is essential in life and career settings.

If you aren't driven by a commercial mindset or to monitor and measure key metrics, reframe by developing a higher motivation to work with money, finances, and the commercial side of products, services, and change.

Reframe by understanding the business proposition for change and innovation.

Build your capability to understand the indicators that are important to measure, and to communicate to influential others who invest in the change strategies you want to create.

DAMAGING PATTERNS OF THINKING
Not knowing what makes you unique and different

DESCRIPTION

Don't be too hard on yourself. Many women were raised to "fit in," be humble, and not stand out! Is it any wonder we aren't practiced in embracing, embodying, and celebrating our differences publicly?

You may not know what makes you different because you have never thought about it or you don't want to embrace your uniqueness completely.

In our work systems and markets, it is important to be able to express your strengths, the value that you are bringing to the team or the process, and the difference that your contributions are making. Taking it one step further, it is increasingly important to be able to describe the value of this difference.

Know how your unique qualities are contributing to others.

Describing the difference will inspire you and others, and is essential to moving others (and yourself) forward.

REFRAME

If you have been hiding your talents, you can reframe by embracing who you are, including your talents and skills.

Find your "people"—those who accept you. Seek feedback on what makes you unique and valuable.

Owning your personal truths, release or reframe any beliefs that limit you.

Reframe any scarcity mindsets that imply that if you stand out you are unsafe, or that your standout behavior is unfair for others around you.

Own your strengths and learn to tell your story of uniqueness and impact.

Assess the context you are in when you are determining and describing your unique value proposition. If it is a job interview, identify the role, the company, and how your strengths and experiences fulfill the company's needs. This requires you to understand the job market and what other candidates can contribute.

If you are describing a new product or a change you are recommending, the process is similar.

Know the customer or stakeholders involved in the change or who will want or be affected by your new product or service.

Understand their "pain points" or needs and describe how you will solve their problem, and why your solution is better than others that could be proposed.

DAMAGING PATTERNS OF THINKING
Not prioritizing what is important, fun, or satisfying

DESCRIPTION
Achieving goals requires you to make choices about where to focus, and to sequence and pace the change so that it is sustainable and satisfying.

Don't underestimate the impact of play, inspiration, and rest and relaxation.

Develop a wellbeing plan so that you are renewed and inspired continuously.

Don't put off what you need or desire until you have advanced and achieved other goals.

Learn to prioritize yourself so you can continue to fuel your readiness to
face and overcome the challenges of change.

REFRAME
Are you exhausted because you aren't prioritizing yourself and your wellbeing?

Are you regularly inspiring yourself?

Are you making the path toward your goals sustainable and playful?

If you aren't leading the change you desire in a way that keeps you satisfied, inspired, and engaged in the process, reframe your mindsets, focus, sequencing, and pace.

Strategies for closing this power gap

To raise your personal power to advance forward, you must understand the natural cycle time for change, projects, tasks, your career, or your business. How many goals are you working on at one time? How often do you move from one task, goal, or project to another? Do you want to move on quickly or do you like things to remain stable for long periods of time? Do your goals require big changes or are you more focused on maintaining the results that you have achieved?

Depending on your preferences, habits, and motivations, you may be motivated or demotivated to use your energy to keep things the same, consistent, and stable, or to lead incremental or radical change. To advance, making this power pivot will require you to be more comfortable leading and managing change, and know the motivations and change preferences of those whom you are leading and collaborating with. You will need to understand how to inspire yourself and them, each step of the way. And you will need to understand the culture and the environment of the change you are leading, including its readiness for change, and whether the change you are creating or the innovation you are designing will be embraced or be sustainable.

If you are in a context that is not going to support you, your leadership style, or the change you are designing, think about changing your context, choosing another context, or reframing your leadership style, communication style, or change strategy. Take time to understand the alignment of your strengths, purpose, and vision for change with the context. You may decide to start up and scale up your change elsewhere. Always consider yourself, your uniqueness, and your value. Design your leadership development journey and your change processes to be inspiring and sustainable, with your wellbeing and the wellbeing of others in mind. Any change starts from the inside out. Reflect, reframe, re-vision, and leverage your results. Align your change and the pace of change with your internal clock and the risk appetite of the organization or system you are working in. Pick your tribe, time, pace, and place for lasting change. Embody, embrace, and celebrate the changes you are leading.

Keys to leading change for your power pivot

Become a master change artist. Connect to your purpose and those who can be influential in supporting the change you desire. Involve them and leverage their support. Understand the value proposition, why the change is needed, and the benefits of the change. Know the risks that come with creating change, including the risk perspectives of others involved in the change. Effective and enduring change can be inspiring and feel like play, or it can feel like a battle with resistance at each step.

Remember that change is an emotional process. Embrace the change process, be prepared for the journey, make it as productive and satisfying as possible, and celebrate each step toward your success. Fully experience the change you create and feel the impact that you make in the world—this fuels the flame and increases your personal power. When you become a master change artist, you can see the cycles of immobility, pain, and self-sabotage, and you can consciously choose a different future. You can choose a new pathway that transforms your inner and outer world.

There are some keys to closing this power gap and making the power pivot to advance yourself and others.

Visualize and strategize

Visualize how you will advance and choose strategies that provide momentum and growth. Here are three key points to remember:

- **Be SMART.** Let your vision lead to **s**pecific, **me**asurable, **a**ttainable, **r**elevant results that can be delivered on a sustainable **t**imeline. Pace yourself. Prioritize. Stay curious and experiment. Understand what could be blocking you and anticipate that you will need to pivot. Reflect and reframe, starting with yourself and your thoughts and beliefs if needed. Consider the people involved. Understand the mindsets of those involved in the change you are leading, and adjust your style and strategies to engage them or to influence them.

- **Know your appetite for risk.** How much risk are you comfortable with in different situations? Know the risk appetite of your culture, team allies, partners, and investors. Consider the investment, risks, and gains that will come from your strategies in the short and long term. Design your transformation and change for sustainability. Expand your appetite for risk when required and be ready to change strategies or pivot if your risk appetite doesn't match the opportunity or challenge in front of you.

- **Know your unique value proposition (UVP).** Do you know what makes you unique, and can you deliver a valuable proposition to those you need to influence or lead? When you do, your confidence, courage, and creativity will flow. To lead, innovate, and influence, you must back yourself, which requires you to embrace your uniqueness and diversity. Take the time to know what makes you and your ideas unique, different, and valuable. You will be called on to express your UVP in meetings, and when setting goals, building a budget and business case, posting on social media, and delegating. Can you express your opinion, take a position, or set a vision and bring yourself and others along on a journey to the end goal? To find and express your UVP, identify what you believe to be true about yourself, an issue, or a project, and describe the importance or value and how this benefits others.

Prioritize fun, satisfaction, and what's important

Masters of change understand that inspiring yourself and others powers up your leadership and influence. Understand what is important to you and others and focus there first. Make the journey toward your vision and your goals fun, rewarding, and satisfying to ensure that you have the personal power and energy to navigate around inevitable challenges. Find your genius flow, which reflects all that motivates you, and use that flow to create momentum to reach your goals.

Celebrate the success you deserve

Do you have a deep-rooted belief that you don't deserve success? The belief that you are not enough or that you do not deserve success creates resistance in yourself and others. Feeling underserving comes from situations in your past that have influenced your outlook. Uncover these memories, emotions, and beliefs, and shift your outlook by working to clear any emotions and beliefs that are stopping you from advancing. Instead, be unstoppable. Embrace and embody these changes in your mindsets, strategies, and results to continue to anchor your feeling of success and to power up your leadership and lift your sense of personal power. Celebrating fills you with positive emotions and inspiration.

POWERFUL QUESTIONS
THAT ACCELERATE YOU!

Before we move on, here are some questions I'd like you to think about:

1   In a few words, describe how you want to feel and show up in the coming year.

2   What are the wildest and most hopeful dreams you have for yourself at this stage in your life or career?

3   What mindsets do you hold that limit you? What mindsets do you want to grow? How will these mindsets advance you toward your goals?

4   What do you want your journey—to advance yourself, career, and business—to look and feel like? How can you design and master the change process to make the journey fun, rewarding, and satisfying?

5   Now you know that your support team is crucial to your success. What support do you need from them? What specifically will you ask them to provide? What is your next step to influence and secure their support?

Power affirmation: I advance toward my vision moment by moment, step by step.

CONCLUSION
A FRAMEWORK TO
ACCELERATE YOU!

"A woman is the full circle. Within her is
the power to create, nurture, and transform."

DIANE MARIECHILD

W E COVERED a lot of ground in this book—well
done for making it this far. Before I leave you,
I want to summarize the *Accelerate You!* framework and explain the inspiration behind it. To do that,
let's take a quick look at modern leadership and the
"ambition revolution" swelling among women.

Modern leadership and the ambition revolution

> "We can start by better defining and modeling ambition for women and girls. We need to ensure that the connotation captures the positives of the concept—making a difference in the world and being one's best self."
>
> **MARY WITTENBERG**

Modern leadership relies on mindsets, self-awareness, and your ability to take yourself and others on a journey toward your goals by harnessing emotions, clarity, confidence, creativity, courage, and the power of trust, belief, and transformational change. Modern leaders must be able to experiment, take risks, leap into the unknown, and adapt to changing circumstances.

Leadership is context-based, which includes the values, relationships, trends, and dynamics of the systems in which you are operating. These contexts are often not equitable. They can be rife with gender bias, with some leaders displaying toxic behaviors, often unconsciously. Developing an awareness of how various leadership styles impact you and others enables you to make conscious choices.

Conscious choices start with understanding leadership archetypes. In their book *Your Unstoppable Greatness*, Lisa Orbe-Austin, PhD, and Richard Orbe-Austin, PhD, describe five toxic leader archetypes: perfectionist, insecure, erratic, withholding, and "prove it to me" bosses. In contrast, leaders who successfully build psychological safety and trust, for themselves and others, consistently offer praise and feedback; promote excellence rather than perfectionism; champion diverse, inclusive, safe environments; focus on developing all employees; and seek to prevent burnout. As we've discussed throughout this book, a focus on self-awareness and wellbeing is essential. Build your ability to be contextually aware and know the importance of assessing "culture fit" so that you can assess, choose, and change your life and work systems, and continue to build and maintain your agency, authority, autonomy, and personal power while helping others to develop theirs.

Self-aware women make conscious choices. Amanda Blesing, in her book *Step Up, Speak Out, Take Charge*, describes the ambition revolution that is swelling in women. This revolution begins with an awakening within, which is leading women to reconceptualize their ambition, question their tolerance of toxic workplace systems, and develop strategies to design their careers on their own terms—taking back their personal power. Within the workplace and society at large, a shift is required to leverage the talents, productivity, positive results, and impact that women bring. New models of leadership are required to redefine and model personal power for women *and* men.

In the meantime, as we work collectively to increase diversity, equity, and inclusion for everyone in the workplace, women are creating their own leadership journeys. Women are stepping into their own power and leading with purpose, passion, and a new paradigm for leadership. And that's where the *Accelerate You!* framework comes into play.

The *Accelerate You!* framework

This framework is evidence-based, tested, and results-oriented, and is designed to be a journey of discovery for leaders who identify as female/women/her/she. *Accelerate You!* enables women to close their power gaps by practicing and integrating new mindsets and capabilities into their lives, careers, and businesses. On this journey, women learn about a variety of modern leadership styles and the gendered mindsets that create the barriers they may encounter. They discover seven strategies they can use to orienteer their pathways:

- Leadership and personal development,
- Self-awareness,
- Resilience,
- Voice and visibility,
- Resources and networks,
- Coaching, and
- Identifying and navigating unconscious gender bias.

As part of this framework, women learn to master change. *Accelerate You!* works with women of any employment status or career stage and accommodates women leading within a variety of organizational sizes and types, in a variety of roles and organizational levels. It was born from the experiences of female leaders in STEM careers employed in the aggressive, male-dominated tech sector that is focused on leading disruptive change through the commercialization of research-based discoveries that use the startup and scaleup pathways.

Starting first with appreciating an individual's strengths, program participants complete a variety of self-reflective exercises and assessments. Each woman is paired with a personal coach and engaged in a personalized debrief on her strengths and power gaps. Participants then select one or more power gaps to focus on during the program. Throughout the program, women participate in peer coaching to help discover their personal truths and vision for their leadership development journey. Peer coaching also supports each woman's pathway to integrate the outcomes and results in closing their power gaps.

One of the individual assessments is Fingerprint for Success (F4S), mentioned in Chapter 2, which illuminates the participants' mindsets so that they can begin to understand their motivations, learn how to develop and expand their repertoire to enable more flexibility in a variety of contexts, and explore and adopt the mindsets that increase their personal power. Using the objective data from F4S, the participants can explore their power gaps. As a recap, the five personal power gaps are:

PERSONAL POWER GAPS

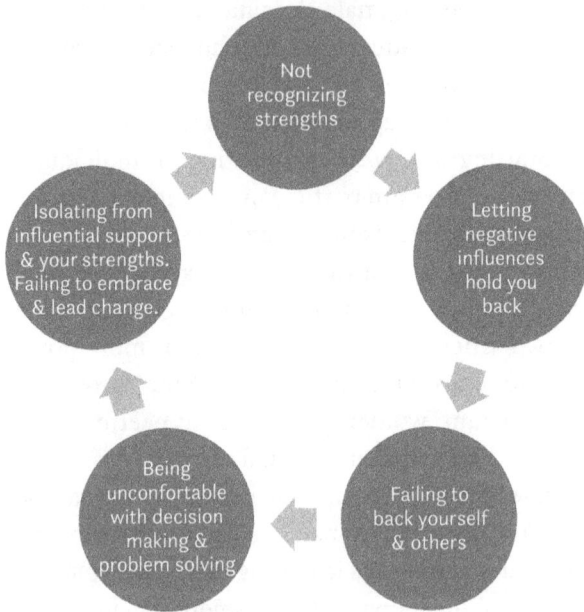

As each participant begins to design their individualized leadership development journey, they proceed to use the five steps, or power pivots, for leadership: awaken, activate, advocate, amplify, and advance. These power pivots are required to close any power gaps and to power up each participant's leadership.

POWER PIVOTS TO CLOSE YOUR POWER GAP

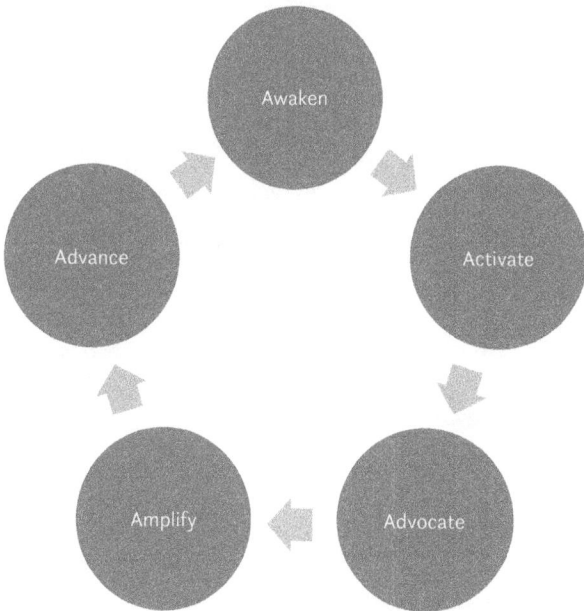

To continue the individualized leadership development journey, each leader will make personal power pivots to strengthen their capability. They will leverage five mindsets: clarity, confidence, courage, creativity, and change. These mindsets are used to enable change and to increase the leader's personal power.

MINDSETS TO CLOSE YOUR POWER GAP

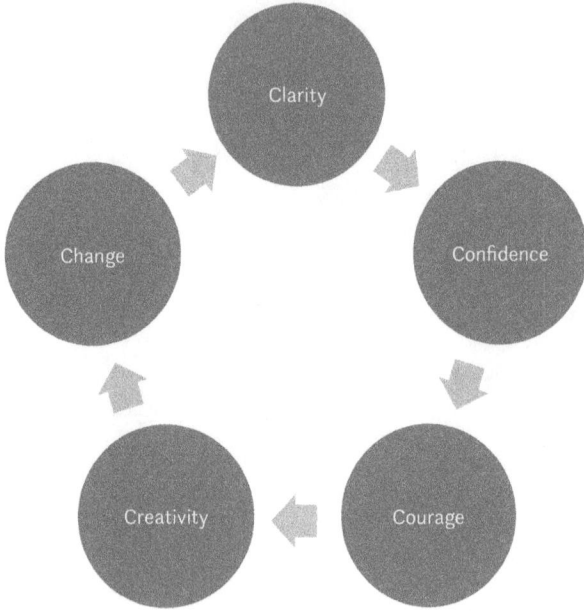

Accelerate You! builds leadership capabilities and is a pathway for women to explore and build their personal power. It requires a woman to be curious, demonstrate radical acceptance, build her connection to her intuition and inner wisdom, and stay connected to her internal and external resources. As a result, it increases her self-compassion, empathy, humility, and her capacity to communicate and collaborate as she masters the change process and develops her own leadership style in a gender-biased world.

ACCELERATE YOU!
LEADERSHIP CAPABILITIES AND PATHWAY

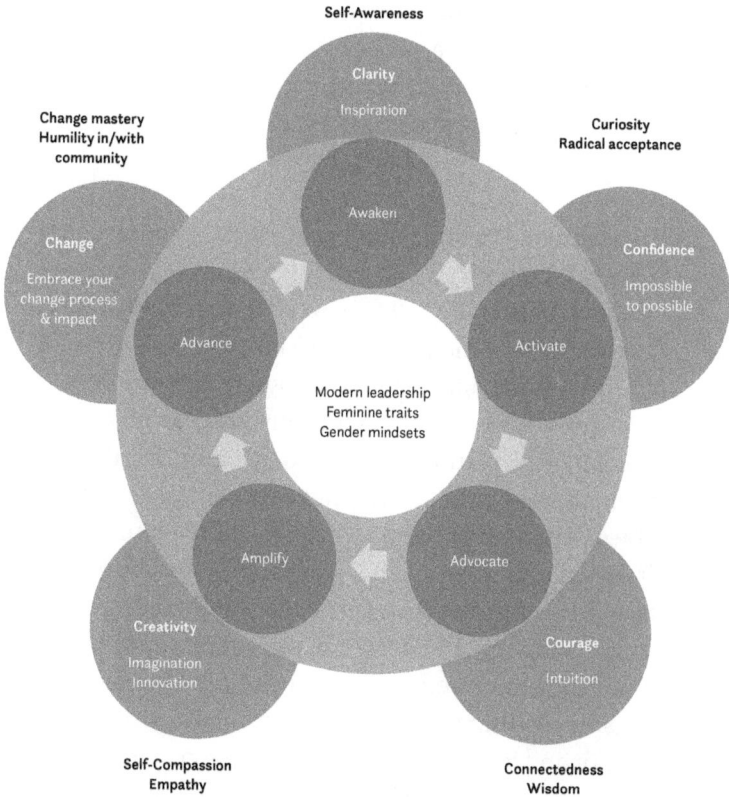

Self-Awareness

Clarity
Inspiration

Change mastery
Humility in/with
community

Curiosity
Radical acceptance

Change
Embrace your
change process
& impact

Awaken

Confidence
Impossible
to possible

Advance

Activate

Modern leadership
Feminine traits
Gender mindsets

Amplify

Advocate

Creativity
Imagination
Innovation

Courage
Intuition

Self-Compassion
Empathy

Connectedness
Wisdom

This program can be effective for individual women joining the *Accelerate You!* learning community or for organizations that are interested in offering a development pathway within their organization. For more information about this framework, visit www.JeriChilders.com.

My quest to *Accelerate You!*

"To all the little girls… never doubt that
you are valuable, powerful, and deserving of
every chance and opportunity in the world
to pursue and achieve your dreams."

HILLARY CLINTON

I was inspired to bring *Accelerate You!* to life because I know from experience and my research the challenges of designing a life, career, and business in a world that is inequitable and biased. I have felt the frustration and challenged myself to create my own power pivots throughout my process of personal transformation. I have used the *Accelerate You!* framework to move my feelings of powerlessness to power up my leadership. I have made the journey from waiting to be given a fair go and a seat at the table to leading the change I needed for myself.

Growing up, I had big dreams—most of them innovative or entrepreneurial in nature, although I wouldn't have known that at the time. I was a social warrior and fascinated with science, design, and the process of learning and transforming. I spent hours playing, designing, and inventing, all the while defending the underdog, and calling for some action and change for my latest cause. As I grew older, I was fascinated with how decisions were made, what influenced decisions, how to lead change, and the dynamics of individuals and teams in marketplaces and workplaces.

On my journey, I learned that I love the independence and freedom to choose my adventure of the moment. I developed a mindset of curiosity, even before I knew I would become an academic at a university. These traits enabled me to park popular opinions and rely on my own observations to make sense of the world. This made me seem aloof and a bit of a rebel. I enjoyed leaning into those personas. I would form ideas, begin to test my fledgling theories, develop strategies, and work through my fears or failures. I learn through doing, and relish the process of innovation and transformation.

Accelerate You! means harnessing the mindsets, processes, steps, habits, and artistry of innovators and entrepreneurs to lead for results and impact.

I would like to hear from you about your own heroine journeys. Specifically, how you were able to identify your power gaps, make power pivots, and develop your own power playbooks. Please contact me and tell me about your journey toward clarity, confidence, and courage, and how you have become a creative force in our world, at Jeri@JeriChilders.com.

REFERENCES

Note: References are listed in order of appearance.

INTRODUCTION

Gladys McGarey, 2023, *The well-lived life: A 102-year-old doctor's six secrets to health and happiness at every age*, Penguin Random House UK.

Amy Cuddy and JillEllyn Riley, August 11, 2021, "Why this stage of the pandemic makes us so anxious," *The Washington Post*.

Replicon, May 11, 2022, "17 reasons women make great leaders."

McKinsey & Company, October 18, 2022, "Women in the workplace 2023."

Kathy Caprino, 2020, *The most powerful you: 7 brave paths to building the career of your dreams*, Murdoch Books.

Maureen Murdock, 1990, *The heroine's journey: Woman's quest for wholeness*, Shambhala Publications.

Sarah Durham Wilson, 2022, *Maiden to mother: Unlocking our archetypal journey into the mature feminine*, Sounds True.

Donald Sull, Charles Sull, and Ben Zweig, January 11, 2022, "Toxic culture is driving the great resignation," *MIT Sloan Management Review*.

Donald Sull, Charles Sull, William Cipolli, and Caio Brighenti, March 16, 2022, "Why every leader needs to worry about toxic culture," *MIT Sloan Management Review*.

Ruchika Tulshyan and Jodi-Ann Burey, February 11, 2021, "Stop telling women they have imposter syndrome," *Harvard Business Review*.

Ruchika Tulshyan and Jodi-Ann Burey, July 14, 2021, "End imposter syndrome in your workplace," *Harvard Business Review*.

Ruchika Tulshyan, 2022, *Inclusion on purpose: An intersectional approach to creating a culture of belonging at work*, MIT Press.

Jeri Childers, Tania Machet, and Michelle Duval, 2021, "Women in STEM: How can we understand and support their career development?," *IEEE Frontiers in Education*.

Women Rising, 2023. *The voice of women at work 2023 report*.

Natalia Peart, March 17, 2021, "How diversity and innovation drive great cultures in the future of work," *Forbes*.

Sylvia Ann Hewlett, Melinda Marshall, and Laura Sherbin, December 2013, "How diversity can drive innovation," *Harvard Business Review*.

CHAPTER 1

Julie Diamond, 2016, *Power: A user's guide,* Belly Song Press.

Sharon Melnick, 2022, *In your power: React less, regain control, raise others*, Wiley.

Kathy Caprino, 2020, *The most powerful you: 7 brave paths to building the career of your dreams*, HarperCollins Leadership.

Kemi Nekvapil, 2022, *Power: A woman's guide to living and leading without apology*, Penguin Random House Australia.

Oksana Barsukova, 2016, "Psychological characteristics of an ambitious person," *Journal of Process Management New Technologies,* 4(2): 79-80.

Anna Fels, April 2004, "Do women lack ambition?," *Harvard Business Review*.

Katie Abouzahr, Matt Krentz, Claire Tracey, and Miki Tsusaka, April 5, 2017, "Dispelling the myths of the gender 'ambition gap,'" Boston Consulting Group.

Mihaly Csikszentmihalyi, 2008, *Flow: The psychology of optimal experience*, Harper Perennial.

Margie Warrell, October 30, 2013, "Do you know your 'why?' 4 questions to find your purpose," *Forbes*.

CHAPTER 2

Jeri Childers, Tania Machet, and Michelle Duval, 2021, "Women in STEM: How can we understand and support their career development?," *IEEE Frontiers in Education*.

Carol Dweck, 2017, *Mindset: Changing the way you think to fulfil your potential*, Robinson.

Holly Ransom, 2021, *The leading edge: Dream big, spark change and become the leader the world needs you to be*, Penguin Random House Australia.

Tasha Eurich, January 4, 2018, "What self-awareness really is (and how to cultivate it)," *Harvard Business Review*.

Michelle Duval, 2013, "The success and failure, attitudes and motivations of Australian entrepreneurs and business builders," *University of Derby*.

Startup Genome, 2023, "The global startup ecosystem report 2023," *Startup Genome*.

Jeri Childers, Tania Machet, and Michelle Duval, 2021, "Women in STEM: How can we understand and support their career development?," *IEEE Frontiers in Education*.

Michelle Gibbings, 2018, *Career leap: How to reinvent and liberate your career*, Wiley.

CHAPTER 3

Stephen R. Covey, 1989, *The 7 habits of highly effective people*, Free Press.

Kendra Cherry, 2023, "The unconscious mind, preconscious mind and conscious mind," *Verywell Mind*.

Daniel Goleman, 2005, *Emotional intelligence: Why it can matter more than IQ*, Daniel Goleman.

Matthew D. Lieberman and Naomi I. Eisenberger, 2009, "Pains and pleasures of social life," 323(5916): 890–891. *Science*.

Sofien Gannouni, Arwa Aledaily, Kais Belwafi, and Hatim Aboalsamh, 2021, "Emotion detection using electroencephalography signals and a zero-time windowing-based epoch estimation and relevant electrode identification," 7072, *Scientific Reports*.

Susan David, 2017, *Emotional agility: Get unstuck, embrace change, and thrive in work and life*, Penguin.

Alicia Nortje, May 29, 2020, "Assessing emotional intelligence: 19 valuable scales and PDFs," *PositivePsychology. com*.

Pippa Grange, 2021, *Fear less: How to win your way in work and life*, Vermilion.

CHAPTER 4

Brené Brown, 2016, *Daring greatly: How the courage to be vulnerable transforms the way we live, love, parent, and lead*, Penguin Life.

Brené Brown, 2018, *Dare to lead: Brave work. Tough conversations. Whole hearts.*, Vermilion.

Brené Brown, 2021, *Atlas of the heart: Mapping meaningful connection and the language of human experience*, Vermilion.

Melanie Dean, 2020, *The hidden power of emotions: How to activate your energy field and transform your life*, Hay House.

Carol Dweck, 2017, *Mindset: Changing the way you think to fulfil your potential*, Robinson.

Martin Taylor, 2022, "What does fight, flight, freeze, fawn mean?" *WebMD*.

Cathy Ferringo, 2023, "How to speak without fear—finally speak up with confidence," *Cathy Ferringo Coaching*.

CHAPTER 5

HeatherAsh Amara, 2014, *Warrior goddess training: Become the woman you are meant to be*, Hierophant.

Simon Sinek, September 2009, "How great leaders inspire action," *TEDxPugetSound*.

Simon Sinek, 2011, *Start with why: How great leaders inspire everyone to take action*, Penguin.

Stephanie Burns, May 24, 2021, "What 'finding your why' really means," *Forbes*.

Brené Brown, 2016, *Daring greatly: How the courage to be vulnerable transforms the way we live, love, parent, and lead*, Penguin Life.

CHAPTER 6

Sharon Melnick, 2019, *Success under stress: Powerful tools for staying calm, confident, and productive when the pressure's on*, HarperCollins Leadership.

Lisa Orbe-Austin and Richard Orbe-Austin, 2022, *Your unstoppable greatness: Break free from imposter syndrome, cultivate your agency, and achieve your ultimate career goals*, Ulysses Press.

CHAPTER 7

Kemi Nekvapil, 2022, *The gift of asking: A woman's guide to owning her wants and needs without guilt*, Penguin Random House Australia.

Elizabeth Scott, 2023, "Perfectionism: 10 signs of perfectionist traits," *Verywell Mind*.

Katherine Morgan Schafler, 2023, *The perfectionist's guide to losing control: A path to peace and power*, Orion Spring.

Lisa Orbe-Austin and Richard Orbe-Austin, 2022, *Your unstoppable greatness: Break free of imposter syndrome, cultivate your agency, and achieve your ultimate career goals*, Ulysses Press.

Gabrielle Bernstein, 2018, *Judgment detox: Release the beliefs that hold you back from living a better life*, Simon & Schuster.

Nicole LePera, 2021, *How to do the work: Recognise your patterns, heal from your past, and create your self*, Harper Wave.

Nicole LePera, 2022, *How to meet your self: The workbook for self-discovery*, Harper Wave.

Sarah Woodhouse, 2021, *You're not broken: Break free from trauma and reclaim your life*, Penguin Life.

CHAPTER 8

Brené Brown, March 2012, "Listening to shame," TED.

Brené Brown, July 2021, "We need to talk about shame," TED.

Jeri Childers, 2005, "Research on leadership development: Women's ways of knowing." *Association for Continuing Higher Education annual meeting.*

David L. Cooperrider, Diana Whitney, and Jacqueline M. Stavros, 2018, *The appreciative inquiry handbook: For leaders of change*, Berrett-Koehler Publishers.

Brené Brown, 2015. *Daring greatly: How the courage to be vulnerable transforms the way we live, love, parent, and lead.* Penguin Life.

Howard Love, 2016, *The start-up J curve: The six steps to entrepreneurial success*, Greenleaf Book Group Press.

World Health Organization, 2021, "Promoting well-being."

Kate Bradley, June 28, 2021, *Money mindset: Why it matters and how to improve it.* Being More Human.

American Psychological Association, 2022, "Face the numbers: Moving beyond financial denial." *APA.org.*

Jeri Childers, Tania Machet, and Michelle Duval, 2021, "Women in STEM: How can we understand and support their career development?" *IEEE Frontiers in Education.*

Amy Cuddy, 2016, *Presence: Bringing your boldest self to your biggest challenges*, Little, Brown and Company.

Amanda Blesing, 2019, *Invisible to invincible: A self-promotion handbook for executive women*, BookPOD.

Amanda Blesing, 2017, *Step up, speak out, take charge: A woman's guide to getting ahead in your career*, Global Publishing Group.

Aleksandr Litvinov, thesis publication pending, "Engineering students' experiences of empathy in entrepreneurial pre-accelerators: A hermeneutic phenomenological study." *University of Technology Sydney*.

Kirstin Ferguson, 2023, *Head and heart: The art of modern leadership*, Viking.

CHAPTER 9

Executive Agenda, June 1, 2023, "The 8 best ways to evolve as a leader."

Mark Travers, October 3, 2021. "4 key qualities of balanced people: What it means to be psychologically balanced," *Psychology Today*.

Robin J. Ely, Herminia Ibarra, and Deborah M. Kolb, 2011, "Taking gender into account: Theory and design for women's leadership development programs," *Academy of Management Learning & Education*, 10(3), 474–493.

Karen S. Lyness and Donna E. Thompson, 2000, "Climbing the corporate ladder: Do female and male executives follow the same route?," *Journal of Applied Psychology*, 85(1), 86–101.

Herminia Ibarra, 1993, "Personal networks of women and minorities in management: A conceptual framework," *The Academy of Management Review*, 18(1), 56–87.

Alice Eagly and Linda L. Carli, September 2007, "Women and the labyrinth of leadership," *Harvard Business Review*.

Anna Fels, April 2004, "Do women lack ambition?," *Harvard Business Review*.

Herminia Ibarra, Robin J. Ely, and Deborah M. Kolb, September 2013, "Women rising: The unseen barriers," *Harvard Business Review*.

Herminia Ibarra and Otilia Obodaru, January 2009, Women and the vision thing, *Harvard Business Review*.

Deborah Tannen, September–October 1995, "The power of talk: Who gets heard and why," *Harvard Business Review*.

Jeri Childers, Tania Machet, and Michelle Duval, 2021,
"Women in STEM: How can we understand and support
their career development?," *IEEE Frontiers in Education*.

CONCLUSION

Lisa Orbe-Austin and Richard Orbe-Austin, 2022, *Your unstoppable greatness: Break free from imposter syndrome, cultivate
your agency, and achieve your ultimate career goals*, Ulysses
Press.

Amanda Blesing, 2017, *Step up, speak out, take charge: A
woman's guide to getting ahead in your career*, Global
Publishing Group.

Bonnie Marcus, September 28, 2015, "Do women really want
power?" *Forbes*.

Julie Coffman and Bill Neuenfeldt, June 17, 2014, "Everyday
moments of truth: Frontline managers are key to women's
career aspirations," *Bain & Company*.

Kirstin Ferguson, 2023, *Head and heart: The art of modern leadership*, Viking.

Amy Cuddy, 2016, *Presence: Bringing your boldest self to your
biggest challenges*, Little, Brown and Company.

Kemi Nekvapil, 2022, *Power: A woman's guide to living and
leading without apology*, Penguin Random House Australia.

Michelle McQuaid and Megan Dalla-Camina, 2016, *Lead like
a woman: Your essential guide for career clarity, true confidence, vibrant wellbeing and leadership success*, Michelle
McQuaid and Megan Dalla-Camina.

Brené Brown, 2018, *Dare to lead: Brave work. Tough conversations. Whole hearts.*, Vermilion.

Glennon Doyle, 2020, *Untamed*, The Dial Press.

Andrew Ramsden, Rob Kirby, Feda Adra, David Beal, Cheryl
Cruttenden, Martin Krippner, Andrew Lizzio, Nicky Mih,
Sarah-Jane Peterschlingmann, and John Smilek, 2023,
Wholehearted leadership revolution: Learn how 10 impactful

men and women have disrupted worn out methods to lead through crisis and build momentum, Four Eagles Publishing.

Ruchika Tulshyan, 2022, *Inclusion on purpose: An intersectional approach to creating a culture of belonging at work*, MIT Press.

Abby Wambach, 2019, *Wolfpack: How to come together, unleash our power and change the game*, Piatkus.

ACKNOWLEDGMENTS

THANK YOU TO those of you who have accelerated me forward!

To the women who demonstrated courage to tell the stories of their leadership development journeys—your clarity, confidence, courage, creativity, and willingness to embrace and lead change inspired me!

To my family for their continual support and encouragement, for believing in and supporting my dreams, creative impulses, and my path beyond challenges on my own transformational journey. Your helping hands sustained me.

To Arti Agrawal, Robyn Fitzroy, Yemi Penn, Justine Lawson, and Beata Francis for reviewing early drafts of this book; your feedback and suggestions have made this work better.

To my sailing community—thank you for teaching me about life, leadership, and how to chart a course for adventure!

To the generous, talented women who have
inspired and supported me throughout my career:
Georgia Abbey, Behrokh Abbasnejad, Taran Ahuja,
Imogen Aitkins, Alexis Airey, Arti Agrawal, Tracey
Allen, Myrian Amielh, Laetitia Andrac, Margaret
Atkinson, Lucia Bautista, Jenine Beekhuyzen, Babs
Bengston, Barbara Bennett, Dori Bennett-Lentz, Lau-
ren Black, Lynn Blanchard, Julie Alexander-Bingham,
Emaly Black, Patricia Book, Jacqui Books, Selena
Boyfield, Jo-Ellen Burston, Karen Bruns, Nicky
Cantrell, Katy Campbell, Adriana Carvalho, Honglin
Chen, Eva Cheng, Jane Cockburn, Dina Cooper, Julia
Coyle, Emily Cullen, Elisa-Marie Dumas, Laura Earl,
Megan Elliott, Jami Emerson, Leisa Griffin Field,
Robyn Fitzroy, Beata Francis, Nancy Franklin, Nancy
Franz, Danielle Fryday, Anne Gardner, Brenda Gard-
ner, Sharon Givens, Anna Groenendyk, Simone
Henderson-Smart, Barbara Holland, Patsy Janson,
Margie Janti, Liz Jenkins, Laura Jiew, Faezeh Karimi,
Yvonne Kelly, Elizabeth Krushinskie, Eva Lam Sam,
Justine Lawson, Caroline Lepron-Aguesse, Tracy
Leonberger, Mary Leuci, Natalie Lloyd, Annie Luu,
Grace McCarthy, Mary McGovern, Sarah McLach-
lan, Julia McMillan Fallon, Richelle McNae, Kirsty
McPhail, Nicole Madigan, Maya Marcus, Maritza
Messina, Anne Miles, Suzanne Morse Moomaw,
Sarah Nanclares, Angela Obrien, Nuala O'Donnell,
Kelly Parkes, Simone Paterson, Yemi Penn, Annik
Petrou, Angela Philp, Claire Power, Pam Price, Julia
Prior, Karen Quigley, Judith Ramaley, Lauren Rich-
ardson, Stevie Rocco, Pamela Sable, Bethany Scott,

Negin Shariati, Lisa Sibilia, Aleksandra Skibinska, Tamantha Stutchbury, Sabine Staver, Matija Squire, Cathy Terrens, Joanne Tipper, Elizabeth Tomc, Leesa Tongoulidis, Rhonda Turner, Irene Tsang, Cathy Valentine, Beth Velde, Alice Warren, Heidi Watson-Held, Rachel Weine, Janet Winemiller, Christie Whitehill, Tracey Wickham, Manuela Whitford, Loletta Yuen, and Didar Zowghi, thank you for inspiring me, lifting me, and letting me learn from you.

To the inspiring experts featured in this book, my wonderful coaches, clients, mentees, business partners, course members, students, board members, and colleagues who encouraged me to share my research and stories. It has been an incredible blessing to have known and worked with you.

To my soul mentors, Joan Sabatino, Jo Searles, Stevie Rocco, Haikuin Rose, Paula Wilder, Bridget Simmerman, Amanda Blesing, Michelle Duval, Pip McKay, Andrew Low, Lauren Jobson, and Sheila Vijeyarasa, thank you for your generosity and for sharing your wisdom.

To my beautiful voice coach, Dana Sui Free, who taught me so much and who gave me regular opportunities to sing and raise my voice. Your wisdom rocks me!

To the women's communities and organizations that advance and accelerate women, I am proud to have worked with you to foster positive change in our world while supporting women on transformational journeys. These include Canva, Inspiring Rare Birds, Lift Women, Tech Ready Women Academy,

Friends With Dignity, various programs within the Faculty of Engineering and Information Technology at the University of Technology Sydney (Women in Engineering and IT Program, Advancing Women in Tech Program, Techcelerator, Female Founder Mentoring Program), the University of Wollongong, the Australian National University's College of Engineering, Computing and Cybernetics, and the Commonwealth Scientific and Industrial Research Organisation (CSIRO). I tip my hat to your clarity of vision, confidence, courage, creativity, and for your leadership in designing positive change in the world.

My heart is filled with gratitude for the pioneering women with whom I have conducted research: Tania Machet, PhD, and Michelle Duval, MA.

To all the allies and champions who paved the way for me and other women because it was the right thing to do, I thank you and acknowledge your contributions—you know who you are!

To the Grammar Factory Publishing team, Scott MacMillan, Michelle Stevenson, and Ania Ziemirska, who helped bring to life *Accelerate You!* Thank you for helping me tell my story.

ABOUT THE AUTHOR

"Awaken to your personal power. Advocate
for yourself and your dreams. Learn to Accelerate
You! The world needs your leadership."

JERI CHILDERS, PHD

JERI CHILDERS, PhD, is the
founder of *Accelerate You!*—a
female leadership development
framework. Her company offers
coaching, leadership, and business
development services. Jeri works
with leaders, accelerators, organizations, and communities who want a coach or business catalyst who co-creates with them a customized
roadmap for advancing women in their careers, or
commercial or social impact projects.

Jeri develops leaders and teams with a focus on
mindsets and intentional change strategies that combine mindset research, brain science, and innovation
approaches for leadership and business development.

For more information about Jeri and her online programs, events, mentoring, and coaching services, visit her at www.JeriChilders.com.

Jeri lives in Sydney, Australia and loves yachting, motorcycling, making art, and commercializing ideas that change the world.

To learn more about Jeri's programs, receive free resources, or view her online courses, go to:

www.JeriChilders.com.

You can also connect with Jeri via her social media:

LinkedIn: Jeri Childers

Facebook: Accelerate You!

Instagram: Accelerate You!

X or Twitter: Accelerate You!

Pinterest: Accelerate You!